Defending Public Education

Defending Public Education

When Partisanship, Anarchic Dissent, and Universal Singularity Attack

Jeff Swensson

ROWMAN & LITTLEFIELD
Lanham • Boulder • New York • London

Published by Rowman & Littlefield
An imprint of The Rowman & Littlefield Publishing Group, Inc.
4501 Forbes Boulevard, Suite 200, Lanham, Maryland 20706
www.rowman.com

86-90 Paul Street, London EC2A 4NE, United Kingdom

Copyright © 2024 by Jeff Swensson

All rights reserved. No part of this book may be reproduced in any form or by any electronic or mechanical means, including information storage and retrieval systems, without written permission from the publisher, except by a reviewer who may quote passages in a review.

British Library Cataloguing in Publication Information Available

Library of Congress Cataloging-in-Publication Data

Names: Swensson, Jeff, author.
Title: Defending public education : when partisanship, anarchic dissent, and universal singularity attack / Jeff Swensson.
Description: Lanham : Rowman & Littlefield, [2024] | Includes bibliographical references and index. | Summary: "Throughout this book, proponents of public schools are warned about the intentions and actions of encroaching partisanship designed to demolish the teaching and learning all US students require to exercise intellectual autonomy for successful citizenship and open futures"—Provided by publisher.
Identifiers: LCCN 2023044174 (print) | LCCN 2023044175 (ebook) | ISBN 9781475873818 (cloth) | ISBN 9781475873825 (paperback) | ISBN 9781475873832 (epub)
Subjects: LCSH: Public schools—United States. | Education—United States.
Classification: LCC LA212 .S966 2024 (print) | LCC LA212 (ebook) | DDC 371.010973—dc23/eng/20231214
LC record available at https://lccn.loc.gov/2023044174
LC ebook record available at https://lccn.loc.gov/2023044175

*For Rochelle Ganz Swensson,
and in memory of Glenn Wiemer and Leo Benson:
the finest public educators I've ever known.*

Contents

Prologue	ix
Acknowledgments	xiii
Introduction: Just Look Inside This Book and You Will See . . .	xv
PART I: BALANCE?	**1**
Chapter 1: About Teeter-Totters and Educational Choice	3
Chapter 2: The Common Good	9
Chapter 3: The Best Interests of . . .	13
Chapter 4: Partisanship	23
Chapter 5: I See These Threats Looking at Me	39
Chapter 6: Revolt of the Likeminded	47
PART II: *DEUS EX MACHINA* IN THE SCRIPT FOR PARTISANSHIP	**55**
Chapter 7: Preemptive Censorship	57
Chapter 8: Anarchic Dissent	61
Chapter 9: Rights and US Education	75
PART III: THE FOES OF TRADITIONAL PUBLIC EDUCATION	**85**
Chapter 10: Partisan Education	87

PART IV: RELIGION, COURTS, THE FEDS, AND PUBLIC SCHOOLS — 105

Chapter 11: Evolution—The Faithful Sound the Alarm — 107

Chapter 12: Schools and Rights—Burdens, Exposure, and Compulsory Conduct — 113

Chapter 13: To Reform or Not to Reform? — 125

PART V: US EDUCATION: JOURNEY OR DESTINATION? — 141

Chapter 14: The Compass Rose: Purpose — 143

Chapter 15: To Defend Public Education—Good Dissent — 151

PART VI: ACROSS THE GREAT DIVIDE — 155

Chapter 16: The Chasm — 157

Chapter 17: Critical Questions — 161

Epilogue — 169

References — 171

Index — 181

About the Author — 185

Prologue

Public education in the twenty-first century is under siege. Assailed by local and national groups, bashed by political action committees, maligned by ideologues, and assaulted by enraged individuals, public schools, public educators, and public school boards are subjected to unrelenting recriminations.

Maybe public educators and those who value traditional public education should have seen the attack coming, but several distractions intervened:

1. Teaching and learning are difficult; focused on the learning needs of all students, public educators have time for little else.
2. National surveys regularly confirm that Americans, especially parents and caregivers, are satisfied with the public school their child attends.
3. The pandemic sent educators and families into a full-court-press to provide learning while mitigating the impact of the virus on students.

Focusing on the student-centric purpose of public education and working to sustain the purpose of public schools (teaching students *how to think* on behalf of the common good), public educators were blindsided by a horde of enraged partisans.

The attack on traditional public education often involves verbal or written condemnation of the purpose and practices of everyday teaching and learning. Imagine serving as a public educator and receiving a written communication like this:

To: (Reader's name here)
Fr: (P. Artisson)
Re: Your Public School Doesn't Do What I Want It To

After touring Open Futures Elementary School, I'm angry and disgusted. I saw first-grade students reading books that they selected for themselves in the library. Do you know where those books came from and whether parents approve of them?

I also heard a fifth-grade teacher sharing a lesson about the Civil War. She said that slavery was one of the causes of the Civil War. I don't think that's right. We should not teach our students things that make them uncomfortable.

And, in third grade there was a student sitting on what looked like a giant beach ball instead of a chair. How can that be right? My elementary school was very orderly, and students sat in rows in every classroom. At your school, I didn't see one classroom that looked like that.

Besides, I saw students sitting beside each other that really have no business being side by side. I never went to school with those students. Besides, they can't learn.

What I saw should not happen in our public schools. I hope you change the school and do what I think students deserve. I am sure that if you do not do what is best, the new school board members that I helped elect will.

Angry and accusatory communications (represented by this imaginary correspondence) are a regular part of traditional public education in the twenty-first century. Vitriolic messages demand that *partisanship* should be imposed on teaching and learning. Proponents of partisanship (defined here as dedication to closely held beliefs derived from a blend of ideology and faith) insist that educators and officials act to meet their demands to reform traditional public education.

Communications and actions directed at demolishing the current purpose and practices of public schools are initiated by individuals, organizations, political action committees, and legislatures. These actors intend to upset the contemporary ideological- and belief-neutral balance of teaching and learning in public schools. To overturn the educational status quo, proponents of partisanship employ disruption, dissent, and denial.

Public educators, parents/caregivers, and other citizens who support public schools face an intense assault. At first, this attack on traditional public education surprised many public educators and those who support public schools. But they should have seen it coming.

On the verge of the twenty-first century, Sikkink called attention to a "divide between the intimate, normative relations of the family sphere and the formal, professional logic of the educational sphere. This structural divide may increase the extent that public schools are seen as hostile to individual moral and spiritual values" (1999, p. 53).

A more accurate prediction about US education in the twenty-first century is hard to imagine. A structural divide continues to separate the two major perspectives about America's schooling: traditional public education and partisan education. Normative relations between the family sphere and the formal sphere of traditional public education are out of balance; hostility reigns.

Balance is an outcome sought by the proponents of traditional public schools *and* the opponents of traditional public schools who advocate for *partisan education*. But balance is not defined similarly by the proponents of these two major perspectives about US education. Traditional public education pursues its purpose to prepare students to navigate *precarious-balance*. Partisan education pursues its purpose to imbue students with capacities required to maintain *static-balance*.

Advocates of partisan education perceive static-balance as the guarantor of social reality aligned with closely held beliefs. Advocates of traditional public education perceive that navigating precarious-balance is the ability that students require in contemporary social reality.

One way to imagine the line at which contemporary US education divides is in the depiction of education as a positional good: "'The value of a person's education depends not only on how good it is an [sic] absolute terms, but on how good it is compared to that of other people'" (Marples, 2014, p. 30). Adherents of the two major perspectives battle over the value of education in both absolute and comparative terms.

Disparate intentions and outcomes for teaching, learning, and social reality are reflected in how balance is defined, accessed, and implemented. Dynamically opposed iterations of balance reveal each perspective's impetus for control of education, citizenship, government, and individual rights.

Static-balance represents the absolutist and collectivist imperatives of partisanship. Ideological principles and faith-based tenets coalesce as partisanship for education dedicated to self-aggrandizing practices and outcomes. Static-balance is the destination of partisan education.

To navigate precarious-balance, students experience traditional public education as a journey. Knowing along with others is the baseline of the purpose of public education that engenders intellectual autonomy necessary and sufficient for participatory citizenship.

What will future communications with US educators convey? Will one major perspective or the other prevail to influence the future of learning, citizenship, and government? Is static-balance or precarious-balance in the best interests of students, adults, society, and/or government that works?

The discussion that follows is an examination of the forces and factors that influence the structural split between the two major perspectives about US education. These forces and factors are central to the determination of balance for social reality perched on one side or the other of this divide. Every reader of this discussion is challenged to predict, as Sikkink did, what lies ahead.

Acknowledgments

This book is inspired by the day-to-day professionalism of the millions of adults who dedicate their careers to what's best for all students in traditional public education. Certified and non-certified staff members are difference-makers whose knowledge, skills, and care put students in a position to be successful as individuals and as citizens. Dedicated to the open futures of all students, public educators and traditional public education are the heartbeat of the future of our communities and our constitutional democracy.

I acknowledge the influence of so many researchers, scholars, and educators whose written work challenged my thinking. The ideas and constructs presented within the references utilized in the writing of this book have been transformational. Of course, none of the inspiring colleagues who wrote these resources are responsible for my "take" on their important thinking.

It is necessary, also, to acknowledge the influence of the closed minds of the ideologues and partisans who attack intellectual autonomy and open futures for students in traditional public schools. Discriminatory, often racist, and prodigiously self-centered, the attack on public education is an unconscionable demand that non-partisans abandon their rights and beliefs in favor of partisanship. This revolt of the likeminded demands a persistent, data-based defense of the rights of non-partisans and of the purpose of traditional public education.

Finally, I acknowledge the input of anonymous reviewers who encouraged the pursuit of this discussion. I am grateful for the professional expertise of Charles Harmon and Jasmine Holman from Rowman & Littlefield Publishers. Their efforts were pivotal in bringing this discussion into print.

Finally, this discussion acknowledges the students who attend traditional public education.

Introduction

Just Look Inside This Book and You Will See . . .

This book presents a focus on the structural divide between the two major perspectives about education in twenty-first-century America. Each perspective entails radically different outcomes for students and society.

Learning, curriculum, instruction, ideology, faith, the rule of law, partisanship, parental rights, majority rule, participatory citizenship, constitutional democracy—all are sorted out during this discussion. Investigating the purpose and outcomes of each major perspective, this discussion exposes the choices that will determine control over America's teaching and learning.

Divided into sections composed of chapters, the title of each part provides an overview of the content explored in the chapters that follow:

- Part I: Balance?
- Part II: *Deus Ex Machina* in the Script for Partisanship
- Part III: The Foes of Traditional Public Education
- Part IV: Religion, Courts, the Feds, and Public School
- Part V: US Education: Journey or Destination?
- Part VI: Across the Great Divide

The chapters in each section explore frameworks that play a major role in the contemporary struggle over control of US education:

1. The purpose of education and the outcomes fulfilled by purpose are inextricably linked with the *social reality* envisioned by proponents of the two major perspectives.
2. The nature of learning envisioned by proponents of each perspective cultivates either *universal singularity* or *participatory citizenship*.

3. The role of students during instruction and the role of education in the future of students play out in each perspective as expressions of *closely held beliefs* or *the common good*.
4. Disagreement between the proponents of each major perspective about learning for the role of citizenship pivots on whether "democratic governments necessarily compel their citizens to do things that some people will find objectionable" (Bowie, 2019, p. 10).
5. The nature of dissent is directed, in one way or another, by each perspective about US education. Either *anarchic dissent* or *good dissent* will influence the future of learning, which is the future of citizenship.
6. *Precarious-balance* or *static-balance*, good dissent or anarchic dissent, participatory citizenship or universal singularity are the ends of continuums that set the stage for the defense of, or the attack upon, traditional public education.

The discussion that lies ahead is a caution, a warning, and a call to action for parents/caregivers, citizens, and educators whose dedication to all students is expressed in the intellectual autonomy and open futures required from America's education if constitutional democracy is to thrive.

PART I
Balance?

Chapter 1

About Teeter-Totters and Educational Choice

Every child knows two things about teeter-totters: (1) balancing on a teeter-totter is always a work in progress, and (2) bullies or selfish kids slam their end of the teeter-totter against the ground to eject the kid at the other end.

Teeter-totters give twenty-first-century America a clue about the profound differences between the two major perspectives about US education. Choosing between *traditional public education* and *partisan education*, parents, caregivers, citizens, educators, and public officials will decide either:

- the extent to which US education should prepare students for the work in progress of navigating precarious-balance, or
- the extent to which US education should prepare students to eject knowing along with others in favor of the universal singularity required for static-balance.

Choosing how best to understand balance, and the effect of education on balance as social reality, means considering the individuals most affected: students.

During traditional public education, students create unlimited pathways to the future, including, but certainly not limited to, welder, physician, custodian, musician, teacher, carpenter, coder, firefighter, truck driver, writer, football player, teacher, plumber, actor, salesperson, mechanic, and graphic artist. Of course, pathways can overlap. Welders can be writers. A salesperson can be a carpenter and a coder.

Every student/future adult is smart. "Smart" is not exclusive to any one person, to any one job, or to any one way of thinking and behaving. Smart is fashioned during informal and formal education throughout each individual's lived experiences. But how smart perceives balance suggests the extent to which the structural divide that now splits US schooling is a challenge to the future of constitutional democracy (Natanson, 2023a).

Balance emerges on both sides of this divide when people apply what they have learned about individual rights, compelling interests of government, and participatory citizenship. The iteration of balance sought through one major perspective or the other fashions the behaviors, decisions, and "smart" that yield social reality. And social reality envisioned by advocates of each major perspective about education could not be more dissimilar.

The intersection between student learning and schooling will influence tomorrow's workers, politicians, artists, professionals, farmers, scientists, homemakers, parents/caregivers, entrepreneurs, professionals, and corporate executives. Today's students, also, are tomorrow's voters. What today's students learn will either prompt navigating precarious-balance or imposing static-balance. In turn, one outcome or the other will shape practices, policies, and actions that determine the nation's future social reality.

THE HISTORY OF US EDUCATION IS ITS TOPOGRAPHY

Any discussion about US education deals with an uneven landscape. History depicts an uneven landscape where underfunded and segregated public schools, too often, have buried the hopes of children of color (Lewis, 2012). Public education is a territory beset by inadequacies and tainted by inequities, by resistance to judicial rulings, by financial gerrymandering, and by exclusionary practices (Swensson, Lehman, and Ellis, 2021).

Cratered, the landscape of public education presents barriers to students of color, students whose first language is not English, and students in poverty on their journey of learning. These students too often are separated from the teaching and learning necessary and sufficient to fulfill the promises of US constitutional democracy (Suitts, 2016; Suitts, 2019).

The lay of the land ensures that students from low-wealth communities face daunting obstacles to meaningful and challenging learning for bright futures. Struggling to overcome the imbalance of historic neglect, public educators also contend with efforts to remove, eliminate, or dumb-down the resources and learning experiences available to students (McLaughlin and Hendricks, 2017).

With this panorama as a backdrop, the response to inadequacies—historic and otherwise—is found in stalwart and professional efforts to improve public education. Improvement brings with it a focus on the purpose of public schooling and engagement of all students with this purpose.

The noble purpose of America's public schools—teaching all students *how to think* on behalf of the common good—is aligned with *civic respect*. Neufeld and Davis (2010) identify civic respect as a transformational link between democracy and public education: "Civic respect is a form of recognition respect in that it is a form of respect that is owed to persons in virtue of their standing as free and equal citizens" (p. 97). This connection between citizenship in constitutional democracy and traditional public education is long-standing (Dewey, 1916).

But the purpose that facilitates navigating precarious-balance is not the only vision for social reality that guides US schooling. Sustaining and expanding the structural split is preferred by some parents, caregivers, ideologues, politicians, and citizens. These individuals perceive that public education fails because it is not connected to faith, ideology, and universal singularity which are among the non-negotiable closely held beliefs at the core of partisanship.

Partisans view this failure as traditional public education abandoning an ideology-based and faith-centered ethos that ought to be integral to institutions in the public sector. Enraged, fearful, determined, defiant, and disdainful, citizens who seek to replace contemporary public education with their beliefs about *what is right* and *what is true* turn to partisanship.

The imposition of partisanship on traditional public education is perceived as an irrevocable right and given full-throated expression when:

- A citizen speaking to a Michigan school board "assailed the board both for compulsory masking and for trying to impose C.R.T.'s 'woke ideology'" (Bergner, 2022, para. 16).
- During public comment portions of a local school board meeting, Indiana residents lambasted school district leaders for "topics from diversity and inclusion including books available to students to masks and COVID-19 protocols to social-emotional learning and more" (Slaby, 2022a, p. A2).
- A group calling themselves "Pornography Is Not Education" sued a publisher and the Colorado Library Consortium "claiming that they were knowingly distributing materials that were harmful to minors" (Pekoll, 2020, p. 31).
- A Texas mother "raised the alarm at a board meeting about titles listed as options for her eighth-grade daughter's book club, noting they included strong language" (Richman and Smith, 2022, para. 9).

Without putting too fine a point on it, the proponents of partisanship let loose with the equivalent of a primal scream in defiance of traditional public education. Such is the ferocity of those who raise their voices that only a complete overhaul of public schools will suffice to still their outrage.

For students, each major perspective lies at one end or the other of continuums formed by several arbiters of choice, including *how to think* versus what to think, student-centric education versus adult-centric education, singularity versus the common good, and accountability for all students versus accountability to free market theory (Swensson, 2023).

Arbiters of choice represent continuums that demonstrate the breadth of the structural divide and denote the basis for the struggle to control US education. The significance of this struggle is profound. Learning from the education anchored by one perspective or the other, US students will perceive liberty in one of two ways: *freedom from* government action or freedom *guaranteed by* the obligation of government to act.

PARENTS AND CAREGIVERS

It's not easy to be a parent or caregiver. Parents/caregivers do their best in a world filled with surprises, unknowns, rewards, dangers, successes, and failures.

Some of the inescapable difficulty that comes with being a parent/caregiver arises from the inevitable changes that happen as a child grows up. One of these inevitabilities arrives when a child interacts with people, institutions, and experiences outside the family.

Children learn, at first, *in* a world shaped by the aspirations, ideologies, memories, and beliefs of their parents/caregivers but grow *into* an outside world that some adults perceive as a threat to the expectations and beliefs nurtured by family.

The passage of time brings both celebrations and anxieties as parents/caregivers guide and monitor the lives of their children. Family priorities, beliefs, and expectations are meant to anchor the choices, decisions, and behaviors of children as they grow. The hope and intention of any parent/caregiver is that these expectations and priorities provide a meaningful, enduring foundation throughout a child's life.

Family priorities and beliefs inevitably come face to face with experiences, others, and institutions when children encounter the outside world. If family-based expectations appear to be in danger when offspring grow *into* the world, some parents/caregivers react ferociously.

One of the first experiences that 90 percent of US students have while growing *into* the world is with traditional public education. As such, traditional public education earns the scrutiny and the approbation of some parents/caregivers who perceive teaching and learning in public schools as a threat to closely held beliefs and the right of family adults to sustain their influence over their children under every circumstance.

Fearful of losing control over the identification and provision of what's best for their child, parents/caregivers assail public education for abandoning *what is right* and *what is true*. An assault on public schools in the twenty-first century occurs because public education is perceived as a contradiction of family values and parental rights (Natanson, 2023a).

At the forefront of this attack are ideological principles, free market theory, and faith-based imperatives which constitute the amalgam of closely held beliefs referred to throughout this discussion as *partisanship*.

Contemporary public education is attacked because its purpose—teaching students *how to think* on behalf of the common good—is the antithesis of the ethos for learning intended by parents, caregivers, and ideologues who favor partisanship. Partisanship is invoked to impose the self-selected prerogatives of parents/caregivers throughout public education.

The purpose of traditional public education departs from the expectations of partisans when it engages students with learning that is necessary and sufficient to enact navigate precarious-balance and craft participatory citizenship. At the center of this learning are the capacities of intellectual autonomy that allow all students to become participants in constitutional democracy amid "a fundamental tension within U.S. society—the tension of diversity and unity" (Brantmeier, 2007, p. 5).

Government that works in constitutional democracy (a teeter-totter in its own right) allays this fundamental tension when the capabilities for navigating precarious-balance engage students with the fundamental understanding that

> at the bottom of every plan of self-government is a basic agreement, in which all the citizens have joined, that all matters of public policy shall be decided by corporate action, that such decisions shall be equally binding on all citizens, whether they agree with them or not. (Bowie, 2019, p. 8)

The purpose of traditional public education engages all students with the capabilities for citizenship an evolving relationship between the rights of individuals and the compelling interests of government. Always a work in progress, navigating precarious-balance involves citizens enacting and accepting the binding nature of corporate action undertaken on behalf of the common good. Government that works in a constitutional democracy thrives when citizenship develops under these conditions.

A SMALL PIECE OF DEMOCRACY

Governance of traditional public education symbolizes the keystone in the arch of America's constitutional democracy. School board elections represent the practical, navigational, and dispositional attributes of participatory citizenship. A small piece of democracy, governance of traditional public education is a proving ground for participatory citizenship and for the obligation of government to act.

Each local school board is an example of "delegated state power, and teachers—[are] agents employed by the state" (Salzman, 2022, p. 1074). A board of education, elected by members of the community, governs the purpose of public education.

When millions of educators go to work each day, they engage 90 percent of America's students with learning in traditional public schools (Bindewald, 2015). Public educators facilitate activities, practices, instruction, and school interactions that grow student intelligences necessary for a conjunction between intellectual autonomy and participatory citizenship to foster the capabilities students require to enact open futures.

This is student-centric learning, and it rests on the premise "that children have an interest in becoming autonomous adults, and that developing autonomy requires an education that engages a person with value diversity" (Reich, 2002, p. 454).

In response to the intention of traditional public education to realize this premise for all students, parents/caregivers in the United States indicate strong support for local public schools. One reflection of this support is the fact that 80 percent of US adults "believe that controversial issues such as immigration, the second amendment, and income inequality should be discussed in high schools" (Rubin, 2022, para. 7).

One Indiana parent shared a brief list of the strengths of traditional public education: "Academic excellence for all students, school safety, preparing students for a global workforce, supporting student mental health and wellness, supporting teachers and promoting partnerships" (Slaby, 2022b, para. 2).

Contemporary positive regard for traditional public education mirrors the fact that for more than a century and without a great deal of fuss, citizens gave consent to traditional public schooling at taxpayer expense "indicating they are 'on board' with the mission and approaches of public schools simply because they accept schooling as a societal benefit and do not reject the expectations of schools" (Stitzlein, 2020, p. 355).

Government framed as constitutional democracy has a compelling interest in traditional public education as the means to access this level of understanding and discernment. A constitutional democracy requires "a system of education that prepares children to participate in its processes with understanding and critical judgment" (Curren, 2009, p. 50). Traditional public education prepares all students to be citizens who engage meaningfully in a social reality awash in precarious-balance.

Chapter 2

The Common Good

The common good is the relatively straightforward notion that there are ideas, laws, principles, actions, requirements, and/or decisions that serve the good of citizens per se.

Teaching and learning in traditional public education facilitate the navigation of precarious-balance, a process of evolving mutuality, necessary and sufficient for the common good. The common good is fostered when the rights of individuals are guaranteed in relationship with the compelling interests of government to sustain the rule of law that protects those rights.

To pursue and to exemplify the common good, traditional public schools welcome all students. The common good is served when these future adults engage with the knowledge, skills, and dispositions that foster ethical citizenship, productive economic participation, and respect for the rule of law.

Traditional public education, on the one hand, is the origin of the social consciousness necessary and sufficient for constitutional democracy because intellectual autonomy and the social reality expressed in the exercise of the common good are not exclusive to one single group, or self-defined cohort, of US students and their families.

Education infused with partisanship, on the other hand, is a negative reaction to the common good. Partisans perceive that traditional public education compels parents and caregivers to send their children to classrooms where closely held family beliefs are abandoned.

Partisans assert the right to impose the principles of partisanship and the tenets of a comprehensive doctrine on public education to rectify the untenable purpose and practices of these *government schools*. If there is a banner headline proclaiming the inviolability claimed by partisans for their closely held beliefs, it is announced in all caps: *parental rights*.

Chapter 2

THE RULE OF LAW

The rule of law is fundamental to the republican form of self-government in the United States. Also fundamental to self-government is the understanding that "workable legislatures must have the power to compel political minorities to subsidize the legislatures vision of the general welfare. James Madison called this elementary power the 'republican principle'" (Bowie, 2019, p. 46).

The rule of law applies to everyone; all individuals and all classes of citizens are subject to the expectations established as the rule of law. The rule of law means that the arbitrary use of power is subordinated to the exercise of well-defined laws. The rule of law is essential to the common good.

Just as no special class of citizens is granted the right to supersede the rule of law, no closely held beliefs of a single cohort or class of citizens is fostered through teaching and learning in traditional public education. This corollary ensures that traditional public education is not beholden to enact or express any one ideology or faith. Traditional public education engages all enrolled students in a faith- and ideology-neutral learning environment.

The rule of law is featured in public schools as part of citizenship education. Preventing the imposition of partisanship, public schools shield students from indoctrination, inculcation, or demagoguery while equipping them with the intellectual autonomy required to support the rule of law and abide by Madison's "republican principle."

Moreover, the purpose of public schooling guarantees, first, that students' personal closely held beliefs are vouchsafed and, second, that students can make sense of challenges, contradictions, and opportunities presented by the outside world.

Public schools engage all students with the capabilities required to enact the processes that sustain the relationship between individual rights and the compelling interests of government. Constitutional democracy thrives when this relationship thrives.

The rule of law, undergirded by the purpose of traditional public education, regulates the heartbeat of citizenship to navigate precarious-balance embedded in the processes and outcomes of constitutional democracy. Without an educational system purposed to ensure citizens capable of navigating precarious-balance, however, participatory citizenship founders, government cannot work, and constitutional democracy atrophies (Bowie, 2019; Marples, 2014).

Echoing Madison, the argument is made that *government could not work* "without the ability to compel people to do or pay for things for which they object" (Bowie, 2019, p. 37).

The question that confronts both public educators and proponents of partisanship becomes: What sort of society, what sort of citizenship, and what sort of social reality emerges if government cannot work? What is the nature of balance if schools do not engage all students with citizenship education?

These questions bring this discussion back to teeter-totters. When teeter-totters are fun, they allow each participant to enjoy collaboration and interaction that comes from a "common good," negotiating a balance while astride the teeter-totter. But teeter-totters are not fun when the only goal of one participant is to eject the other.

ABOUT FREE MARKET EDUCATION

During the latter part of the twentieth century and the initial decades of the twenty-first century, advocates of free market theory brought participant-ejection to the teeter-totter of public education (Chubb and Moe, 1990).

Initially, Friedman (1955) gave voice to choosing between various free market mechanisms. Free market theory inspired partisanship that equated US education with static-balance: efficiency, low-cost, and a divorce from governmental influence. Tilting toward ideological principles and free market mechanisms as tantamount to an adequate education, free market adherents prioritized ideology as the cornerstone of reform for US schooling (Chubb and Moe, 1990; Hess, 2010; Shaw, 2010).

Comparing ideological imperatives with the perceived failures of traditional public education—less government versus government intrusion, efficiency versus bureaucracy, low-cost versus tax burdens, singularity versus mutuality, competition versus the common good—free market proponents leverage the ideological certainties on the left end of these duos as proof of the need to dismantle traditional public schooling (Swensson, Ellis, and Shaffer, 2019a; Swensson, Ellis, and Shaffer, 2019b).

ABOUT-FACE IN THE MARKETPLACE

Slamming one end of the teeter-totter to the ground was not, however, the first choice of advocates for schooling tied to free market theory. In the beginning, marketplace ideas were promoted to improve traditional public schools.

Early intentions for charter schools, for instance, were that they would serve as laboratories from which innovations for teaching and learning in traditional public schools would emerge (Schneider, 2019). The free market's penchant for competition was proposed as the lever that would spur the improvement of public schools. Free market adherents claimed that competition with free market schools would force public educators to fight to keep up.

Albert Shanker, president of the American Federation of Teachers during the 1970s, proposed that charter schools should be "a new kind of public school where teachers could experiment with fresh and innovative ways of reaching students" (Kahlenberg and Potter, 2014, para. 1). Marketplace education enthusiasts imagined that if parents/caregivers were free to choose what was best for their child, they would leave a public school to attend the ideologically aligned, and therefore superior, charter school.

An exodus from public schools to charters, where students would thrive because of superior practices, purposes, and outcomes, would force traditional public schools to abandon the status quo.

These predictions, and the optimism of some early advocates of free market schooling, evaporated as free market proponents turned improvement for public education on its head. Partisanship took hold when advocates of a free marketplace for US education envisioned the eradication of traditional public schools as the way to eliminate the sclerotic bureaucracy and union-domination at their core (Chubb and Moe, 1990).

Proponents of free market schooling engineered an about-face: from improvement to demolition. In the twenty-first century, partisanship continues to march away from the purpose and practices of traditional public education.

For example, teacher unions are condemned "as a well-funded enemy that promotes radical classroom lessons on race and sexuality" (Binkley and Carr Smyth, 2022, para. 12). Observers identify this transformation as part of America's drift "towards more polarization, more partisanship, and non-partisan local politics is part of that trend" (Richman and Smith, 2022, para. 14).

At the forefront of partisanship is *singularity* (Swensson, 2023). Singularity is partisanship's fixation on the supremacy of individual needs and rights. The marketplace operationalized by free market theory facilitates singularity when it chooses *which* individuals deserve to succeed in education and in life. Singularity attenuates marketplace schooling from concern for the common good (Swensson, 2023).

Tenets of free market theory generate static-balance for its own sake; partisanship is festooned with the intentions of static-balance: winners, losers, competition, and survival of the fittest. Partisanship proponents slam their end of the teeter-totter to the ground to jettison the common good.

Chapter 3

The Best Interests of . . .

The primary objective of parents and caregivers is to act in the best interests of their children. From this foundation, all children grow and build their natural intelligence and lived experiences. Family-based, sincere, and steadfast parental beliefs serve a child's best interest as the foundation of informal education.

As this relationship extends through time, it is commemorated during the trials, celebrations, tribulations, joys, and anxieties of parenthood. Of course, every parent-child relationship changes and grows over time. Sometimes, parents/caregivers perceive these developments as threats from a tempestuous and contradictory outside world.

Growth, transition, and change are not always comfortable experiences for parents and caregivers. Some parents and caregivers believe that children can attain what is best in their lives only when standing forever on the foundation of informal education. This conviction holds that no influence, experience, or element in the outside world can be allowed to interfere with the closely held beliefs imparted to their children.

These parents/caregivers assert a right to envelop the lived experiences and the formal education of their child with adult best interests framed by closely held beliefs, family expectations, and ideological premises. The outcomes of informal education and family expectations are held to be one in the same and inviolable (Natanson, 2023a).

INFORMAL AND FORMAL EDUCATION

When parents and caregivers provide mentoring, guidance, love, expectations, and direction for their children, informal education is at work. Informal education (i.e., family-based *comprehensive doctrine*, lived experience, parental expectations) occurs primarily in the earliest years of every child.

Informal education influences each person's natural thinking and individual capabilities.

In the earliest years of a child's life, parents and caregivers properly are in control to nurture and protect and guide. As children grow, and as parents/caregivers continue to guide this growth, formal education and the outside world come alongside informal education.

Formal education provides children with teaching and learning that extends, and adds to, informal education. In so doing, public educators abide by the responsibility to serve the best interests of children. This clarion call reverberates throughout the history of traditional public education; public educators have long served *in loco parentis*.

For more than a century, in fact, formal education mirrored informal education and aligned with the best interests of majority parents/caregivers. For the most part, traditional public schools construed the best interests of students as a combination of basic instruction in subject area disciplines, one-faith allegiance, and celebratory patriotism.

In these simpler times, in an industrial economy, in an analog society, and in a parochial world, the best interests of *all* students in public schools were hardly considered and, in too many instances, completely ignored. Over time, however, aspirations for equity, meaningful implementation of the rule of law and expression of the purpose of traditional public education grew closer to a reality across US society (Levin, 2002; Suitts, 2019).

The extent of this change challenges parents and caregivers who expect public schooling to incorporate their closely held beliefs. From a partisanship point of view, social media, institutions throughout society, and a multitude of additional invaders from the outside world aid and abet traditional public schools and pose a threat to informal education, closely held beliefs, and ideological priorities.

Formal education can challenge, change, contradict, or expand what informal education considers to be inviolable. Formal learning experiences, to the dismay of partisans, engage students with the analytic, practical, emotional, and creative skills, attributes, and dispositions in pursuit of a purpose designed to put every student in position to make sense of the precarious-balance of the outside world in ways that informal education and static-balance do not.

When US public schools engage future citizens with the ideals, ideas, capabilities, and practices of participatory citizenship, and with the intellectual autonomy necessary to navigate precarious-balance, they fulfill "an obligation to expose children to something further, or other, than what they see at home or in their communities" (Wenneborg, 2020, p. 47).

Although exposing students to "something further" reflects the intention to facilitate the capabilities required for success in the outside world, the purpose of public education is perceived as a direct threat to the ethos of partisanship. Public schools, thus, become a source of fear and anxiety for partisan families.

Partisanship comes to school in the demand from some parents/caregivers for the right to sustain their authority over a child's closely held beliefs. For partisans, merely taking authority over their own children is not enough. To ensure absolute control, partisans insist that schooling cannot veer from requiring all students to learn steadfast allegiance to and application of the principles, tenets, and expectations of partisanship.

In contrast, traditional public education is the obligation to provide students with the cognitive and personal wherewithal to exercise individual rights while abiding by the responsibilities of citizenship and the compelling interests of government in a constitutional democracy.

For partisan parents/caregivers, this symbolizes the troubling difference between informal and formal education. Because traditional public education signals a child's initial steps into the outside world and because this world involves interaction with others and their ideas, control may slip from parents' hands. Partisans inveigh against traditional public education because it decreases the locus of control of parents/caregivers and increases interactions with and expressions from a social reality imbued with the precarious-balance inherent in non-partisan principles and beliefs.

The contemporary imbroglio over control of education in America reflects the assertion that the parental right to control informal education is transferable to formal education. Power and control granted by the ideological touchstones in partisanship are identified as rights that partisan parents, caregivers, and ideologues will not relinquish.

Traditional public education, as a result, is recognized as a barrier to parental control, a threat to ideology, and the end of static-balance. Public schools are a formidable obstacle to the tenets and principles of partisanship because intellectual autonomy and pursuit of the common good can facilitate the movement of the arc of the moral universe as it bends toward justice.

Partisanship is a resource for parents/caregivers, ideologues, and legislators that identifies who knows better what are best interests when it comes to controlling US education and installing singularity at the core of social reality.

WHO KNOWS BETTER WHAT ARE BEST INTERESTS?

Informal education and parental guidance are tested when children encounter the outside world. To meet this challenge, parents, caregivers, and ideologues join forces in the conviction that family adults are the only viable arbiters of best interests of children.

To ensure that children pass the test of dedication to closely held beliefs, parents, caregivers, and other likeminded individuals organize to thwart the countervailing influences of the outside world and to end the influence of traditional public schools as an enabler of the capabilities required to navigate precarious-balance.

Foundations, networks, political action committees, and social media sites organize in the name of partisanship to impose closely held beliefs on traditional public education. The aspirations, faith, ideologies, expectations, and lived experiences of non-partisans become irrelevant at best and obliterated at worst when traditional public schools are replaced by *partisan education*.

If partisanship knows the best interests of children, then partisan schooling marginalizes the closely held beliefs of countless non-partisan students. One parent's perspective about educational bedrock can be another's quicksand. The best interests of some are not the best interests of everyone.

Nevertheless, control of the best interests of children throughout traditional public education is a right claimed by those whose best interests are realized when partisanship and closely held beliefs are imposed on "others."

Closely Held Beliefs Know Best Interests

Closely held beliefs offered in sectarian education or private schools constitute a readily available option for parents/caregivers who seek an educational setting imbued with all the trappings of partisanship. In these schools, children are wrapped in teaching and learning that mirror the ideological and/or faith-based expectations of partisan parents and caregivers.

But, from the point of view of adults and ideologues invested in partisanship, these educational options are not enough. These choices do not account for everyday worldly interference with closely held beliefs that abound in traditional public schools. Interference with partisan priorities is a threat with the potential to loosen a child's grip on a family's expectations, aspirations, ideologies, and beliefs.

Heeding a call to act when worldly interference upends closely held beliefs, parents, caregivers, and others decry US public education for its abandonment of faith as a core element. Evangelism is steadfast in answering the call to reassert this missing element.

"Christians have a duty to aggressively spread their faith in 'the Good News' of the gospels so that others might also become saved" (Zimmerman, 2002, quoted in Bindewald, 2015, p. 94). For partisans, this comprehensive doctrine requires no other justification for its presence in public schools.

Networks Know Best Interests

Networking is a tool employed by partisans to identify and protect the best interests of children and young people. Collaboration between partisan parents/caregivers and likeminded entities stands up to unwanted interference from the outside world (Cunningham, 2022, para. 3).

Networks and their individual members apply principles and tenets of partisanship as benchmarks to identify the extent to which traditional public education interferes with and countermands partisan priorities.

For instance, in 2021, the Florida Citizens Alliance fought to prevent worldly interference by listing books "they say contain 'indecent and offensive material'—including 'And Tango Makes Three,' about two male penguins who adopt a baby penguin" (Harris and Alter, 2022, para. 14).

This group in the Sunshine State is a paragon of partisanship networking. The Florida Citizens Alliance "has partnerships with over 100 other groups, including Moms for Liberty and Americans for Prosperity Florida, a local branch of a national group founded by the billionaires Charles and David Koch" (Harris and Alter, 2022, para. 11).

A group founded in 1981, The Council for National Policy, has become a conglomeration of likeminded entities and individuals capable of raising substantial funding to support the priorities of partisanship. One of their policy preferences "is taking down public education and replacing it with privatized schools that practice religious-based indoctrination" (Cunningham, 2022, para. 3).

Partisans perceive that the purpose and practices of public schools undermine family beliefs and the right of parents to nurture and protect these beliefs. To advance the self-proclaimed duty and rights embedded in partisanship, networks across the nation prioritize the best interests of partisans for education:

- *Home School Legal Defense Association:* This US organization was "set up with the purpose of supporting fundamentalist Christians—is quite explicit in its aim of protecting children from what it considers to be the pernicious views associated with secular education" (Marples, 2014, 34).
- *Moms for Liberty:* This organization has over two hundred chapters in forty states and is one of the parent organizations created "to fight progressive trends in schools" (Bergner, 2022, para. 4). Leaders of this group "hope to convert brawlish pandemic-era divisions into lasting political power" (Craig, 2021, para. 4). Moms for Liberty filed with the Internal Revenue Service as "a 'social welfare' group structure that allows it substantial leeway to participate in politics, including taking

unlimited sums of dark money and dispensing those dollars in support of favored candidates" (Cunningham, 2022, para. 1).

Partisanship Knows Best Interests

Partisanship is constructed around several assumptions, one of which is that government schools (i.e., traditional public schools) ignore, neglect, or abandon the best interests of students in favor of the best interests of government and/or left-wing political biases (Bergner, 2022).

Partisanship is deployed to neutralize this threat. From the baseline of partisanship, parents, caregivers, and ideologues work to ensure that public schools are not permitted to offer lessons or learning experiences that are "woke," anxiety-producing, disturbing, challenging, or anti-American (Hixenbaugh, 2022).

Partisanship is the lens through which one group of parents/caregivers objected "to fourth-graders being taught how to spell 'spinal tap,' 'isolation' and 'quarantine' because they were too 'scary of words' [sic] to teach at that grade level" (Craig, 2021, para. 7).

The best interests of partisanship, brewing since the middle of the twentieth century, foment an intentional crisis in US public education. On the brink of the twenty-first century, this crisis was summarized as a "social conflict over public schools [that] is structured by disagreements over the relation of morality, values, and public schools" (Sikkink, 1999, p. 52).

This social conflict is a crisis of perspective about US education that pits the beliefs, faith, and priorities of societal isolationists (those ideologues devoted to free market principles) alongside parents/caregivers convinced of the absolutist nature of their personal proclivities, against the secular and rational ethos of traditional public education (Bindewald, 2015).

US EDUCATION KNOWS BEST INTERESTS

Since its inception in the 1830s, US public education has been a forum meant to focus on nurturing the best interests of students.

For decades, the best interests of children in public school were represented in a static-balance between learning sufficient for gainful employment and closely held beliefs of white, mostly middle-class families (Swensson and Shaffer, 2020). Too often, this meant that the best interests of all students were not the focus of US public education.

In retrospect, any past claim that US education served the best interests of all students is ironic. Attending to the best interests of an exclusive cohort of students, public schools ignored the closely held beliefs and religious principles of many US children and families. The best interests of all students, alongside social justice, participatory citizenship, and constitutional democracy, wobbled under the weight of the irony of public schools representing the beliefs and priorities of only a portion of America's public.

Claiming dedication to the best interests of children, but slanting toward closely held beliefs and ideologies of partisanship for more than a century, traditional public education sustained static-balance while significant portions of its enrollment—families and students of color and in poverty—knew that if this represented what's best then it was a partisanship "best" intended to toss them off the teeter-totter.

FOLLOWING A LONG ARC TO BEST INTERESTS

When best interests were defined in public education by closely held beliefs and majority privilege, an historic incompleteness ran rampant through teaching and learning. Attending to static-balance, many traditional public schools let purpose atrophy. Some students thrived under these circumstances but too often the purported best interests of students transformed the American Dream into an illusion for students of color (Lewis, 2012).

Implementing the purpose of traditional public education and aligning classroom practices with this purpose proved to be a daunting task. Nevertheless, adherents of traditional public education and its purpose persevered.

Public educators, parents/caregivers, jurists, scholars, legislators, and some civic leaders struggled to improve traditional public education, and, consequently, American society, into alignment with the glacial movement of the long arc of the moral universe as it bends toward justice (Parker, nd).

Slowly, tireless efforts moved traditional public education away from limitation, restriction, and adherence with closely held beliefs. The best interests of students, thus, moved along the arc of the moral universe toward the principles at the heart of the common good and the American Dream (Swensson, Ellis, and Shaffer, 2019a).

The common good eschews partisanship as a balkanization of faith, thinking, and action imposed as if these ideological proclivities are necessary and sufficient for learning. The common good nurtures individual expression and dignity alongside the benefits of collaboration, mutual benefit, and interpersonal respect.

The common good depends on individual compliance with social structures that interweave individual rights and compelling interests of the state. In this way, the best interests of children grow and develop in formal education that is unencumbered by faith, ideology, or partisanship. The common good repels coercion intended to remake education in the image of partisan criteria that ought to have no place in traditional public education.

Disrupting the Arc

But long-standing centrifugal forces in American society toss aside the common good and swing schooling toward the principles of partisanship. For instance, after *Brown v. Board of Education* (1956), when traditional public education was prodded to move toward equity, inclusion, and justice, strident voices from some in US society called for schools to pull away from this judicial "push" toward the common good (Levin, 2002; Suitts, 2019).

Appalled with sustained progress toward serving the best interests of *all* students, partisanship erupted, spewing exclusionary ideology and closely held belief across the landscape of traditional public education in the twenty-first century (Pendarkar, 2022).

Mandates for masks, social distancing, and school closures during the COVID-19 pandemic enflamed partisan antipathy for traditional public education and allowed ideologues to double-down on the dangers inherent in the *obligation of* government to act.

Public school compliance with pandemic requirements was decried as government intrusion in matters and issues reserved exclusively for parent/caregiver decision-making. There is no justice, from a partisan's perspective, in intrusion that gives public educators the power to trample "Liberty" and individual rights. Taking umbrage at the common good, contemporary partisanship impedes movement along the arc of the moral universe.

Public educators face the molten fury of partisans opposed to being told what to do by the government. Pushing back against this denial of singularity, partisans lean into their support for schooling intertwined with faith and ideology. Partisans determine that traditional public education is a losing proposition that must be transformed. The foes of public education turn to a marketplace metaphor to promote the total transformation of public schools.

IT'S NOT EDUCATION; IT'S SHOPPING!

From the perspective of proponents of partisanship, contemporary public schools have turned away from the ideological imperatives of singularity, exclusion, and restriction. As if to emphasize how public education offers little or nothing to partisans, *shopping* becomes the metaphor of first resort for partisans who seek to restore static-balance in, and as an outcome of, US education.

Shopping is a benign metaphor that hides the exclusionary and self-aggrandizing ethos of partisanship. On the face of it, this metaphor tells the public that the marketplace is egalitarian. After all, anyone can go shopping. A functioning educational marketplace is ballyhooed by partisans as the place where all the ideological elements required for static-balance are available to any interested party.

This partisan point of view fails, however, to include *caveat emptor* in the fine print. Shopping in the educational marketplace, it turns out, is not open to all potential customers. Discrimination and exclusion pervade the marketplace because the otherwise quotidian shopping metaphor obscures the fact that the "public responsibility for education is replaced by consumer relations" (Gunzenhauser and Hyde, 2007, p. 494).

Consumer relations allow the manipulation of educational choice. Offered as if it's a shopping experience for one and all, educational choice is designed to fulfill the self-interests of partisans to the exclusion of "others."

The tenets of partisanship exclude potential buyers from purchasing the available goods. For instance, vouchers offer state funding to partisanship schools where students can be denied enrollment because "of their or their parents' sexual orientation or gender identity" and/or because they "aren't a 'good fit'" (Hinnefeld, 2023a, para. 1).

The marketplace of educational choice is available primarily to serve the closely held beliefs of partisan shoppers. Shopping is open to eligible, motivated devotees of partisanship to acquire the ideological and faith-centered "items" that are not available from the shelves of traditional public education.

Consumer relations prioritize partisan education and reduce traditional public schools to the role of a second-rate, discount provider barred from the marketplace.

In the educational marketplace, *boutique-ideology* is sold under the partisanship brand name. Boutique-ideology is the term used during this discussion to describe the ideological- and faith-based ethos that infuses partisanship. Boutique-ideology sold in the educational marketplace is a guarantee to partisan shoppers that they can buy teaching and learning aligned with closely held beliefs, parental rights, and informal education.

Education in thrall to free market theory "generally places less emphasis on the perspectives of marginalized peoples, removes suggested discussions of racism and its lingering effects, and promotes the workings of the free market, with limited government intervention" (Natanson and Asbury, 2022, para. 4). Boutique-ideology satisfies those shoppers who want to buy schooling that restricts what is taught and who is taught.

In the marketplace, partisan shoppers can select products (i.e., mechanisms such as charter schools or virtual schools) that fulfill ideological priorities and faith-centered tenets. Shopping for education becomes, via consumer relations, synonymous with identifying and providing for the best interests of partisans.

BUYING BEST INTERESTS: BOUTIQUE-IDEOLOGY

Depicting education as if it's shopping—a simple matter of finding goods with ideologically desirable "function," "ingredients," and "price"—puts the essence of partisanship front and center for parents/caregivers.

Pre-approved shoppers are enticed with opportunities to buy what suits their closely held beliefs without regard for the beliefs or expectations of other students and families and with appreciation for the fact that these "others" can be excluded from shopping in the first place.

Partisans, foes of traditional public education, use consumer relations to claim that the demise of public schools is required to open a marketplace where parents and caregivers can shop for schooling that serves the best interests of their children.

Ignoring the best interests of non-partisan children, ignoring the best interests in the common good, and ignoring the best interests of constitutional democracy, free market shopping is the precursor of schooling that serves the best interests of partisanship. Partisanship adds its weight to the educational teeter-totter to control US schooling.

Chapter 4

Partisanship

Partisanship is "prejudice in favor of a particular cause" (*New Oxford American Dictionary*). The particular cause favored by partisan education is boutique-ideology. Boutique-ideology is a prejudice in favor of *universal singularity* as social reality.

Partisans see education through a spyglass—a monocular view focused on the sole object of value on the horizon, boutique-ideology. Prejudice in favor of boutique-ideology serves the best interests of partisanship. With this objective in sight, partisans direct their energies to the manipulations of schooling required to arrive at this destination.

THE WAY THINGS WERE IS THE WAY THEY'RE SUPPOSED TO BE

Opponents of public education in the twenty-first century look at traditional public education and recoil. From this perspective, traditional public education is out of sync with self-aggrandizing principles and faith-based tenets. Public educators are perceived as forsaking partisanship in lieu of and in response to the misguided and wayward cultural and demographic evolution ravaging the contemporary American landscape.

Partisans yearn for the halcyon days when public schools seamlessly connected with principles and tenets of partisanship (Klicka and Phillips, 1997). These principles, aligned with closely held beliefs of majority families, played an historic role in public education.

Often, adult memories about public school experiences conjure up the equivalent of a Little Red School House. Friends on the playground, memorizing facts, kindly teachers, and lunch in the cafeteria—adults bask in the memory of a safe harbor anchored by a reassuring connection with static-balance anchored by family expectations and closely held beliefs.

For partisans, these remembrances of education suffice as the best representation of the public sector and the promises of the American Dream. Memories woven into past experiences with and practices of public schools inspire allegiance to partisanship. Partisanship represents an opportunity to revive adult best interests in present-day public education where everything fondly remembered seems to have gone astray.

For partisans, the American Dream requires likeminded adults to restore education anchored in the past. Returning to boutique-ideology, teaching and learning will revert to willful ignorance of the failures in US history (e.g., racism, poverty, violence, ethnic/religious discrimination). This exclusionary and absolutist version of the American Dream is nothing less than the resumption of education that imposes the baleful influence of closely held beliefs on the lives and futures of US students.

Reverting to these good old days in education is represented by one of the goals of Restoration PAC, one of the networks emphasizing the goals of partisanship. Restoration PAC "wants to bring the country back to its 'timeless foundation' of 'turning to God and the enforcement of just laws'" (Mansfield and Jimenez, 2022, para. 5).

Hearkening back to educational practices that accommodate boutique-ideology, partisans assault the purpose of traditional public education because learning *how to think* on behalf of the common good erodes "foundational meaning perspectives [which] are developed in early childhood from our most important authority figures" (Hoggan and Kloubert, 2020, p. 297).

Partisans intend to enshrine boutique-ideology in US schooling. What is labeled as dedication to the best interests of children is merely a return to the comfort zone of partisanship.

The past becomes a shield that partisans use to ward off the purpose of public education and safeguard parental rights. Perceived as a disaster in the making in the middle of the twentieth century, the purpose and practices of traditional public schools became a calamity for partisan parents and caregivers during the early decades of the twenty-first century. Partisan angst flourishes in reaction to the extent to which traditional public education strays from closely held beliefs.

WHEN ENOUGH IS ENOUGH

At the height of the COVID-19 pandemic between 2019 and 2021, traditional public education, for all intents and purposes, came to a standstill. Teaching and learning were forced away from schools, out of classrooms, and into cyberspace. Educators and public school parents/caregivers did what they could to engage their students with the purpose of traditional public education.

For eighteen months, and sometimes longer, public schools were closed in the hope of limiting transmission of the virus. Online instruction became the norm and family schedules and student motivation, not to mention parents' patience, paid a price. Anxiety, frustration, and fatigue during the pandemic were exacerbated by an initial lack of knowledge about the virus and confusing directions from government health agencies.

The Center for Reinventing Public Education documented student reactions to pandemic-disrupted schooling. "Students said they were struggling with school and missed their friends and teachers. And they didn't like being on the computer for hours on end" (Chu and DeArmond, 2021, para. 3).

When many public schools slowly resumed normal operations at some point during the 2021/2022 school year, vaccines had been developed for most age groups, hospitals had been overwhelmed, the virus had killed more than one million Americans, and the nation's economy was in disarray.

As the nation struggled to adjust in the aftermath of the pandemic, so did traditional public education. Exacerbating the difficulties of a return to in-class learning, there were current events and the responses to them (i.e., "protests for racial justice, a contentious presidential election, and a riot at the Capitol" [Chu and DeArmond, 2021, para. 1]) that left students and public educators entangled in multiple unresolved issues, concerns, and emotions.

In this post-pandemic educational and societal environment, serious and profound learning losses were reported throughout US public schools. "Negative effects were more pronounced for girls and for young people from marginalized groups, including immigrants, LGBTQ youth, young people of color, and those living in low-income households" (Chu and DeArmond, 2021, para. 4).

Public educators attempted to remedy these deficits and bring student learning back to pre-pandemic levels. Initially these efforts brought mixed results. "Many high-income students were able to limit their learning losses, but on average, low-income students stayed remote longer and lost more ground for each week of remote school" (Friedman, 2022, para. 12).

In the aftermath of the pandemic, partisans unleashed a fusillade of anger at traditional public schools about online learning, school closings, health-related mandates, and government intrusion on the rights of parents and caregivers. Public education practices, boards of education, and public educators were bombarded with accusations, invective, and recriminations.

Rallying against government schools, partisans used the closely held principles and priorities of partisanship as ideological cudgels:

- *Less government:* Federal health guidelines designed to mitigate the health crisis and assist public schools with re-opening—mask mandates, social distancing, and vaccinations—were assailed by partisans as government intrusion (Natanson, 2023a).
- *Parental rights:* A Florida legislator depicted the enforcement of mask mandates instituted in public school districts in no uncertain terms: "We had a wave in school districts that spit in parents' faces" (Atterbury, 2022, para. 4). For partisans, parental rights are sacrosanct.
- *Indoctrination:* The unjustified intrusion of government in public schools, according to partisans, obliterates the right of parents to control everything their children experience. Teaching, thereby, becomes indoctrination when public educators explore concepts, ideas, historical events, and other topics that contradict, challenge, or deny the validity or accuracy of principles or tenets of partisanship. Partisans assail traditional public education and, in so doing, claim that public schools harm children (Lennox, 2021).

Outrage over pandemic-related precautions morphed into a full-scale assault on traditional public education as government-intrusion into private lives. Deciding enough is enough, partisans—parents/caregivers, families, citizens, and ideologues dedicated to partisanship—led the charge to undermine and reform public schooling.

THE FLY IN THE OINTMENT FOR PARTISANSHIP: LEARNING

Partisans yearn for schooling dedicated to their preferred vision of social reality. But, as will be discussed shortly, the transformation of public education, the evolution of US society, and court rulings stand in the way of schooling devoted to boutique-ideology. As if these developments were not devastating enough, partisanship has no real non-ideological answer for the conundrum of learning.

Learning is the purposeful complexity of formal education provided in traditional public schools (Swensson, 2023). Children and young people in K-12 public schools learn knowledge, skills, practical matters, creativity, respect, cooperation, and numerous other dispositions to facilitate their success in society. Learning is the complexity with which students shape and adapt their adult futures.

Learning is a dilemma for partisanship, however, because learning is hard to control. Learning develops a range of capabilities with the potential to negate the limitation, restriction, and exclusion riveted to ideological priorities. These priorities have little to do with the universe of discourse explored in public school classrooms because partisanship is self-limiting.

Partisanship education accommodates neither the universe of discourse nor the complexity of learning. Learning is the fly in the ointment for partisans because instead of a destination suited to static-balance, learning is its own reflection of the immense scale of the universe of discourse as depicted in a small sample of relevant scholarship:

- "Education can be characterized as *initiation into practices that express human flourishing*" (emphasis original) (Curren, 2009, p. 52).
- Good thinking is "the tendency to identify and investigate problems, to probe assumptions, to seek reasons, and to be reflective" (Perkins and Tishman, 2016, quoted in Swensson and Lehman, 2021, p. 144).
- Sternberg, Reznitskaya, and Jarvin (2007) "observe that 'wise thinking involves the ability to use one's intelligence in the service of a common good by balancing one's own interests with those of other people and of a broader community over both the short- and long-terms' (p. 150)" (Swensson, Ellis, and Shaffer, 2019b, p. 19).
- "Meaning-making is 'a developmental measure of how individuals organize their experience, which evolves over time'" (Ignelzi, 2000, p. 10, quoted in Swensson, Ellis and Shaffer, 2019a, p. 26).
- "Intelligence as the global or composite capacity of an individual to act purposefully, to think rationally, and to deal effectively with the surroundings or situation" (Labby, Lunenburg, and Slate, 2012, p. 3).
- "Salovey and Mayer (1990) coined the term 'emotional intelligence' and defined it as 'the ability to monitor one's own and others' feelings, to discriminate among them, and to use this information to guide one's thinking and actions' (p. 189)" (Labby, Lunenburg, and Slate, 2012, p. 3).
- Learning is defined as "the student's power of cognitive ownership" (Swensson and Shaffer, 2020, p. 68).
- Public educators accept the obligation to "prepare all students to recognize and accept the basic equality among all persons, even as the achievement of this imperative is always a work in progress" (Reimers, 2006, p. 282).
- "A good public school prepares students for the 'unfixed' social world for which young people will be learning" (McWilliam, 2008, p. 264).
- "Develop in young people both the knowledge and skills that individuals need to live free lives and the shared values . . . that citizens need to support the institutions that enable them to live freely" (Gutmann and Ben-Porah, 2015, p. 1).

Learning, moreover, befuddles partisans because it often entails what educators call *difficult knowledge* (Hartsfield and Kimmel, 2020). There are, for example, instances from US history that demonstrate unethical, racist, violent, and/or illegal decisions and behaviors. Many other topics constitute difficult knowledge "such as sexuality, sex, racism, death, poverty, and violence" (Britzman, 1998; Robinson, 2013, quoted in Hartsfield and Kimmel, 2020, p. 420).

To deal with difficult knowledge, to embrace participatory citizenship, to understand controversies and conflicts in the outside world, and/or to accommodate lived experiences, learning for all students is the focus of traditional public education. However, for partisanship, learning, difficult knowledge, and preparation for an "unfixed" social reality are the equivalent of bugs in software or wrenches in machinery.

When hobbled by these and other factors, partisanship cannot function. When partisanship cannot flourish in education, the restoration of its ideology- and faith-based precepts becomes job number one for the foes of traditional public education.

WHERE LEARNING THRIVES

By contrast, learning in traditional public education is ideology- and faith-neutral. Curriculum and instruction in traditional public schools are not an attempt to alter or change or destroy the belief system or faith of any student.

Rather, curriculum and instruction in public schools engage all students with learning throughout the universe of discourse to enrich their lived experience, to build on the foundation of their informal education, to acquire the wherewithal to make sense of the outside world, and to put themselves in position to contribute meaningfully to their own success and to the success of their citizenship in the nation's constitutional democracy.

In public education classrooms, intellectual autonomy is the learning outcome meant to put every student in position for an open future where participatory citizenship, economic well-being, and personal fulfillment evolve alongside the dynamic and expanding universe of discourse.

Curriculum in traditional public schools is the guide for learning through which students gain access to the universe of discourse. "A curriculum, which is a set of teaching and learning prescriptions, is in essence a knowledge-forming activity" (Scott, 2014, p. 14).

The curriculum outlines cognitive pathways for teaching and learning that fulfill the purpose of traditional public education. During the years spent exploring these pathways, students are on a journey that equips them with the intellectual autonomy necessary and sufficient to make sense of encounters with challenges, opportunities, interactions, changes, and decisions that lie in their future.

A high school junior in Tennessee spoke to the value of seeing the outside world through the lens of complex learning in traditional public education: "School gave me a broader perspective, as well as the ability to formulate my own views and opinions. Sheltering today's youth from these important issues doesn't make them go away" (Napolitano, 2022, para. 8).

PARTISANSHIP CAN'T FUNCTION

Because learning is multifaceted, because learning facilitates meaning-making in an unfixed social world, because learning is derived from engagement with the universe of discourse, and because public education does not conform to restrictions of boutique-ideology, partisanship cannot function unless public education is reconfigured.

The purpose and practices of traditional public education in twenty-first-century America threaten partisanship because learning can turn obedience to ideology and one-faith into a choice instead of an obligation. Reacting to such educational apostasy, partisans assail traditional public education for its misguided purpose and non-partisan outcomes. Partisanship functions when both faith and ideology fuel curriculum and instruction. To repair function, one-faith education, first, must be restored.

REPAIRING FUNCTION: ONE-FAITH EDUCATION

In a pluralistic society, one faith is, literally, one among many. In a constitutional democracy, church and state, ostensibly, are separate. Partisan demands for an exclusively one-faith public education sparked by dominionism, fundamentalism, and evangelism contradict this social reality in twenty-first-century America. Nevertheless, partisans intend to reunite one faith with public schools to revitalize partisanship function.

As one observer illustrates, the work of partisans to install fundamentalist Christianity in public schools is an attempt to "undermine the teaching of evolution so that creationism may be preserved, promote their faith through school-sponsored prayer and devotional Bible reading, [and] censor textbooks and library materials to prevent students from being exposed to alternative viewpoints" (Bindewald, 2015, p. 107).

Of course, a plethora of religiously affiliated private schools exist in the twenty-first century, and these institutions are free to teach and express faith as they see fit. Vouchers—funded by tax dollars—are available to families in Indiana, for instance, who wish to educate their children according to their faith (Hinnefeld, 2023b).

The existence of these purely sectarian schools, for which financial support from the state is possible, does not deter partisans from demanding that traditional public education also focus on one faith. Partisanship functions best when unchallenged. Reinstalling one-faith as the centerpiece of traditional public education eliminates a significant contemporary challenge to the function of partisanship.

REPAIRING FUNCTION: PUSH BACK AGAINST THE ARC

Partisanship does not function when the arc of the moral universe bends, however slowly, toward justice. Justice is an all-encompassing construct that overwhelms the imposition of closely held beliefs, singularity, competition, and privilege in the public sector that is required if partisanship is to function.

To repair the functioning of partisanship in traditional public education demands that foes of public schooling push back against teaching and learning that equips all students with capabilities that prompt the movement of the arc toward justice. Evidence of the movement toward justice in public education, however glacial it may be, is a disconcerting development and partisans are compelled to push back.

To grease the engine of push back, partisans enact legislation that prohibits instruction about difficult, troubling, controversial, or uncomfortable topics (Lehrer-Small, 2023; Mervosh, 2022). Especially anguish-generating for partisans is instruction that deals with incidents, decisions, or trends in US history that illuminate failure to live up to the promises of America's founding principles.

Eliminating this instruction from public education is one way to ensure that the limited realm of learning prescribed by partisanship is installed in public schools (Richman and Smith, 2022). Another way to bring the restrictions of partisanship to public education is to attack and eliminate straw men like critical race theory (CRT).

The CRT Straw Man

Partisans direct considerable enmity at CRT. CRT "is an academic concept which elaborates on the systemic nature of racism" (Pendharkar, 2022, para. 3). CRT has been singled out as partisan enemy number one for censure and elimination.

Public educators and scholars are quick to point out that CRT is not taught in K-12 public school classrooms (Kingkade and Hixenbaugh, 2021; Pendharkar, 2022). This disclaimer is often followed with the accurate explanation that CRT is a conceptual framework used in some college courses to examine the endemic nature of racism in US society and throughout US history.

Despite evidence that public schools do not teach CRT, partisans wave this "bloody flag" in front of parents and caregivers. If CRT hysteria does not rally family adults to the cause of partisanship, other public school programs such as social-emotional learning (SEL) are condemned as gateways to, or mirror images of, CRT.

Disparagement of CRT, animosity directed at CRT, and fear induced by CRT incite some parents, caregivers, and citizens. Although CRT plays no role in traditional public school curriculum, partisans choose hysteria and outrage in response to reports of its presence:

- In Virginia, at an anti-CRT event organized by a group known as Parents Against Critical Theory, violence broke out and two parents were arrested (Sollenberger, 2021).
- The founder of a group known as No Left Turn "said schools are 'indoctrinating' kids with CRT, 'literally making them your brownshirt'" (Sollenberger, 2021, para. 16).

Partisans choose to push back against real or invented examples of curriculum and instruction in public schools that can be accused of countermanding ideological and faith-based priorities. Allegations, falsehoods, and innuendos about public schools are powered by the partisan premise that boutique-ideology serves the best interests of children.

This premise is blind to the extent to which partisan priorities place little emphasis on academic achievement or concerns for others. Ignoring or defaming public education's positive impact on students, adult-centric objectives take center stage in partisan education.

Partisanship is rooted in understanding that the interests of children are served when free market theory, faith-infused learning, and/or self-aggrandizement are prioritized to train pre-approved students to survive the brutal competition in life's marketplace.

Asserting that the best interests of children are well-served when partisanship suffuses teaching and learning, partisans confirm for each other that push back against public schools is guided by a noble intent. But partisans have only one interest when boutique-ideology is foisted upon America's schools: adult-centric education (Swensson and Shaffer, 2020).

ADULT-CENTRIC EDUCATION

Adult-centric education is the oxymoron that upends intellectual autonomy, open futures, and the purpose of public schooling. Adult-centric education limits and restricts teaching and learning to achieve the outcomes of partisanship. Adult-centric education is teaching and learning that maneuvers student learning to a destination devoid of intellectual autonomy.

Adult-centric education takes guidance, knowledge, encouragement, curiosity, investigation, unknowns, and wonder into a realm of lowest common denominator learning where students frequently have few options for thinking beyond pre-digested academic pablum. The oxymoron of adult-centric education for children and young people turns the challenges, joy, and individual fulfillment of learning for an unfixed world into rigid patterns of thought that lead to preconceived outcomes.

Adult-centric education is the educational environment in which teaching and learning are subservient to ideological and faith-based imperatives. Adult-centric education is fueled by closely held beliefs. From this foundation, partisanship builds schooling where, for example, there is little need to engage students with *how to think* about the relevance and meaning of difficult knowledge from US history.

Partisans reject instructional practices and curriculum topics that explore the universe of discourse because these classroom experiences are harmful and guilt-inducing. Partisans impose severe limits on classroom discussion about episodes in America's history that they deem difficult or "uncomfortable." Among other threats to partisanship, these episodes corrode the shiny allure of boutique-ideology and celebratory patriotism.

Examples from US history of discrimination, hate, violence, or disdain for the rule of law, eligible for exorcism from curriculum and instruction could include:

- Discrimination directed against Mormons, Catholics, and Jews;
- Exclusion directed at Irish, Asian, and Hispanic immigrants;
- Racism directed toward African Americans and Native Americans; and
- Restrictions on rights for women.

The blend of ideology and faith in partisan education does not engage students with investigations about how best to avoid repeating America's historic failures. Partisan education is similarly less inclined to engage students with the ethics and the meaning of the rule of law in government that works for America's constitutional democracy.

Partisanship maximizes the priorities, garnished with celebratory patriotism, that skew teaching and learning toward adult-centric outcomes. Voucher proponents, for example, confirm "that vouchers are necessary to realize the liberty interests of parents in directing the upbringing of their children" (Tang, 2018, 392).

Hinnefeld (2023a) shines a spotlight on adult-centric education engendered by partisanship when he observes that "supporters say vouchers promote 'freedom' because students choose their schools. In fact, schools choose their students" (para. 4). Partisan schools are so closely held that non-partisans are excluded and the needs of "others" are ignored because they have no relationship with the best interests of adult-centric education.

Lashing out against public schools nationwide, partisans complain about mask mandates and COVID-19 vaccines (Terruso and Hanna, 2021), decry CRT as brainwashing (Sollenberger, 2021), and allege that public educators are "grooming" students during lessons about gender-based health issues.

PARTISANS RECOIL

Partisans recoil when closely held beliefs and celebratory patriotism are not the end-all and be-all of teaching and learning in public schools. Partisans attempt to slap the veneer of their beliefs, biases, and prejudices on top of teaching and learning in public schools to prevent the curriculum from exploring indignities, violence, and discrimination in America's history. Difficult knowledge, after all, can make partisans uncomfortable.

On a national level, the 1776 Project political action committee offers one example of efforts to restrict learning in public school classrooms. The 1776 Project political action committee inveighs against teaching CRT and "the group targets almost any teaching about racism and diversity. The group also dabbles in attacking topics related to transgender rights" (Mansfield and Jimenez, 2022, para. 2).

A plan released by a candidate for US president in 2024 reflects the intentions of partisan antipathy toward public education when it "calls for cutting federal funding for any school or program that includes 'critical race theory, gender ideology, or other inappropriate racial, sexual, or political content onto our children'" (McGraw, 2023, para. 2).

Ideologues pile on so that students in public school classrooms are defenseless against the less-than-tender mercies of mandates and imperatives derived from ideological priorities (i.e., standardized testing, test prep instruction, book censorship, restricted discussion topics).

FOR PARTISANS, THE PRESENT IS DOWNRIGHT SCARY

Learning about the common good sustained in the relationship between individual rights and the compelling interests of government is not a priority of adult-centric education. The moral obligations of traditional public education often conflict with the interests of partisans (Swensson and Lehman, 2021).

Contemporary America and traditional public education frighten partisans. Their monocular perspective reveals frightening demographics that are harbingers of the rejection of boutique-ideology. In fear of losing, partisans in the twenty-first century prioritize schooling that rejects the evolving and diversifying expressions of America.

Partisans identify multiple threatening trends. As of 2018, for example, the majority of students in traditional public schools (almost 55 percent) "included several cohorts of America's children and young people: Black, Hispanic, Asian/Pacific Islander, American Indian/Alaska Native, and students of two or more races" (Chen, 2018, quoted in Swensson and Shaffer, 2020, p. 5).

Across the United States, in addition, "diverse ethnic groups have contributed to its religious diversity" (Eck, 2001; Kosmin & Lachman, 1993; Marshall, 2006; Pew Research Religion & Public Life Project, 2013, quoted in Marshall, 2014, p. 140).

These examples of evolving demographics across the United States are not lost on partisans and raise an alarm about the fact that "once there was a Protestant Christian majority [in the United States], but that majority has been shrinking every year" (Marshall, 2014, p. 140).

Contemporary trends in American society put partisans on the defensive. When present-day public education welcomes all students, prioritizes diversity, and substantiates the value of the common good, partisans see the abandonment of closely held beliefs and the denigration of the rights of those who adhere to partisanship. If contemporary public educators and their allies prevail, the worldview embraced by partisanship, and intended as a remedy for the ills of public school classrooms, will lose.

Under these conditions, partisans risk being pushed out of a marketplace winner's circle of their own making. To defeat public education whose purpose and practices relegate boutique-ideology to the close-out aisle, partisans adopt strategies linked to their priorities.

CERTAINTY ABOUT WHAT THERE IS TO FEAR

A categorical distance exists between public education and schooling oriented by partisanship. Sikkink (1999, p. 56) poses a question that suggests the implications of this gap: "How are lifeworld and system (as cultural categories) constructed within religious and other social groups, and how does that construction shape alienation from public schools?"

Partisanship certainties construct a definitive lifeworld and system. These certainties, when adopted by parents and caregivers, are cultural categories that shape alienation from public education in several ways:

- Public education is demonized because it is a secular, rational, faith-neutral, and pluralistic entity detached from and opposed to the private lifeworld of family and faith (Bindewald, 2015).
- Public education earns the antipathy of partisans whose interpretations of the First Amendment decry the government-dependent structure of public schools. Partisans interpret freedom of speech and freedom of religion as *unlimited* individual rights. Partisans perceive the purpose and practices of traditional public education as the abridgment of these rights because public schools prioritize neither partisanship nor partisans and represent a reciprocal relationship between individual rights and the compelling interests of government.
- Partisans perceive that public education is "indoctrination rather than emancipatory education, and anyone on the receiving end of it is justified in feeling disrespected" (Hoggan and Kloubert, 2020, p. 300).
- Partisanship is the lens that parents and caregivers use to focus on their worldview as the social structure that is (1) the sole viable representation of America's social reality, (2) the comprehensive domain that public education abandoned, and (3) the vanguard of ideology and faith required to prioritize singularity as the impetus for imposing a partisanship ethos throughout schooling, society, and democracy.

Partisans Can See Clearly Now

Alarmed by societal change, dismayed by government intrusion, and motivated to restore a preferred past, partisans level a host of accusations at traditional public education. Through the lens of partisanship, parents, caregivers, and ideologues see fearful attributes embedded in the purpose and practices of traditional public education:

- *Indoctrination:* Parents/caregivers and allied organizations claim that public education exists to indoctrinate students. Opponents of traditional public education accuse "public education of indoctrinating students on the basis of race, and then making the same accusation that they are indoctrinating them with LGBTQ propaganda" (Mervosh, 2022, para. 10).

  A slide projected during a Moms for Liberty meeting in 2021 "claimed that 'globalists, utopians, socialists, totalitarians and the UN are using public schools to undermine freedom and Christianity'" (Little, 2021, para. 3).

  Indoctrination, partisans claim, is insinuated into the lives and learning of students when public educators employ two teaching strategies:
  - *SEL*—SEL is condemned as nothing more than a stalking horse for CRT. But public educators and scholars indicate that SEL has nothing to do with indoctrination. SEL is defended as an effective resource for public educators because "student success in school and beyond depends on more than academics; it also depends on developing a healthy identity, self-management skills, self-awareness, empathy, and supportive relationships" (Chu and DeArmond, 2021, para. 1).
  - *CRT*—CRT, a theoretical construct utilized at the university level to examine the history of systemic racial inequality in the United States, serves as an ideological boogeyman. CRT was labeled by a president's Executive Order "as a 'malign ideology that undermines the inherent equality of every individual in America'" (Conway, 2022, p. 712). Some media outlets amplified this perspective and accused teachers in cities on the west coast of being trained by individuals who believe "public schools are guilty of 'the spirit murdering of Black and brown children'" (Bergner, 2022, para. 3). But curriculum documents, lesson plans, and other written materials demonstrate that CRT is not taught in traditional public schools (McGraw, 2023). However, viewed through the lens of partisanship, the mere specter of CRT initiates condemnation of traditional public education.
- *Grooming:* Some foes of public schools claim that public educators groom children and young adults for abuse (Mervosh, 2022; Willen, 2022). False, slanderous statements from partisans accuse public educators of being pedophiles who use their lessons and positions of authority to prepare students for their sexual designs. Horrific claims like these are resolutely denied by those falsely accused. Nevertheless, partisanship and fear rivet this accusation to the framework of public education.

To the extent that these falsehoods demonstrate abandonment of closely held beliefs and the best interests of partisanship, these dangers are rendered inseparable from traditional public schools.

Partisan adults believe—without any evidence except fears plumbed from the depth of partisanship—that the safety of children is at risk because traditional public schools have allowed the tenets and principles of faith and ideology to atrophy.

The all-in commitments that define partisanship ensure that true believers have no interest in heeding the advice of scholars who observe that it's prudent "to step away from the fueling of fear because people can very easily go down a rabbit hole of engaging in debates that become echo chambers" (Pendharkar, 2022, para. 6).

Chapter 5

I See These Threats Looking at Me

Allegiance to tenets of faith and to principles of ideology is the unbreakable foundation upon which partisanship rests. Existential threats to partisan education, therefore, are those ideas and practices that deny the viability of closely held beliefs and undercut allegiance to what is true and what is right from the partisanship perspective.

To deflect and thwart the threats that stalk them, partisans insulate students from the influence of intellectual autonomy. Intellectual autonomy is an existential threat to "Liberty" because partisan learning embraces only tenets of faith and principles of ideology. Although "Liberty" is a right claimed by partisans, "Liberty" does not allow students to question, investigate, or abandon closely held beliefs in favor of intellectual autonomy.

INTELLECTUAL AUTONOMY

Antipathy toward the purpose of public education and disdain for the outcomes students acquire from engagement with learning in public schools is fueled by partisan fear mongering about the intent and outcomes of learning in traditional public education (Richman and Smith, 2022, para. 10).

The purpose of traditional public education engages all students with intelligences (i.e., analytical, practical, creative, emotional) necessary and sufficient for intellectual autonomy. Contrary to the fears of partisans, *how to think* does not mandate rejection of personal and family-expected convictions or beliefs. Rather, "autonomy means providing an environment where choice is meaningful, where opportunities to lead one kind of life or another are real options" (Reich, 2002, p. 456).

Intellectual autonomy is a focus on "fostering the skills and habits whereby learners assess arguments, negotiate their own purposes, values, and meanings, become more aware and critically reflective of assumptions, and become more able to fully and freely participate in discourse" (Hoggan and Kloubert, 2020, p. 301).

Court decisions, particularly those that deal with cases in which book censorship is involved, reflect the role and the effects of intellectual autonomy in traditional public education as these skills and habits develop from curriculum, instruction, and reading during learning experiences in classrooms and in school libraries.

The value of intellectual autonomy as it arises from reading experiences has been validated in several court judgments. For instance, *Minarcini v. Strongsville City School District* (1976) affirmed that school libraries are important privileges that function as a knowledge repository for all students (McLaughlin and Hendricks, 2017).

Almost twenty years after this decision, a district court validated the inclusion of a book in a school library that a board of education removed. In *Case v. Unified School District* (1995), "the school board, the court determined, removed the book because of its disapproval of the content, not because it was educationally unsound or vulgar" (McLaughlin and Hendricks, 2017, p. 10).

A different district court, in Massachusetts, went further to acknowledge the role of literature in learning as a source of discovery and as a resource for valuable exploration:

> The court deemed the library as a place where students 'can literally explore the unknown . . . discover areas of interest and thought not covered by the prescribed curriculum [and] test or expand upon ideas presented to them' (*Right to Read Defense Committee v. School Committee of the City of Chelsea,* 1978, p. 14). (McLaughlin and Hendricks, 2017, p. 10)

Researchers, the judiciary, educators, and parents/caregivers interpret intellectual autonomy as nothing less than the improvement and growth of meaning-making and "wise thinking" for each student (Sternberg, Reznitskaya, and Jarvin, 2007).

Intellectual autonomy, as Reich (2002) observes, "is connected to pluralism" (p. 456). Pluralism, of course, is multicultural, multiethnic, diversely religious, and expressive of innumerable opinions, perspectives, ideologies, and political persuasions.

Intellectual autonomy is the engine that powers every individual's freedom to make meaningful choices in a social reality where participatory citizenship, concern for others, and the compelling interests of government represent pluralism in conjunction with interactions and processes necessary and sufficient for navigating precarious-balance.

The point of learning in public schools is to engage students with *how to think* so that they may steer "a course for one's life through significant choices among diverse and valuable options" (Reich, 2002, p. 456). This is a description of meaningful choices facilitated through intellectual autonomy. All of which means that, for partisans, intellectual autonomy is a threat to certainty.

Although intellectual autonomy is neither an intention nor a guarantee that a learner's future thinking, decisions, or actions will turn away from closely held beliefs, opponents of public schools anticipate the worst from the open futures that are powered by intellectual autonomy.

Intellectual autonomy, pluralism, and the purpose of traditional public education are perceived as devious intrusions on individual perceptions of, and faithful allegiance to, dominionism, fundamentalism, and/or evangelism. Nonconformance with such closely held beliefs is a learning outcome that stymies partisanship. If partisanship is to function, it requires schooling in which students are led to ideological compliance.

COMPELLING STATE INTEREST

In addition to the danger presented by intellectual autonomy, partisans face threats from the compelling interests of government. Despite evidence of the contrary illustrated by two different court cases, partisans perceive the compelling interests of government as unjust intrusions on rights and closely held beliefs.

One of these examples demonstrates the protection of closely held beliefs even though the government claimed a compelling interest. When the US Supreme Court decided *State of Wisconsin v. Jonas Yoder et al.* (1972), "it concluded that the benefits accrued by students in secondary school to be effective citizens and self-sufficient individuals were not great enough to outweigh the substantial burden imposed upon the Amish by compulsory attendance laws" (Reich, 2002, p. 446).

Yoder did not blindly uphold the government's compelling interest. On the contrary, this decision is a determination that the free exercise rights of the Amish were impinged upon by the state's compelling interest in compulsory education.

On the flip side of this coin, the US Court of Appeals (*Mozert v. Hawkins*) found that a school district's use of a specific reading program did not interfere with the free expression rights of the Fundamentalist Christians who bought suit against the school district over the reading program.

The court ruled that "exposure to diverse ways of life and beliefs . . . was not compulsion to believe anything and therefore did not interfere with the parents' freedom to practice their religion" (Reich, 2002, p. 447).

Distinct from *Wisconsin v. Yoder*, *Mozert v. Hawkins* hinges on the finding that a specific element of instruction implemented to fulfill the goals and purposes of a school district curriculum does not interfere with free expression. The reading program, the court found, neither "entailed affirmation or denial of a religious belief, [nor] performance or non-performance of a religious exercise or practice" (Reich, 2002, p. 447).

The instructional program, the court indicated, did not enforce or compel action and, further, constituted only *exposure*. Exposure was found not to constitute a burden on the right to free expression of religion. The government's compelling interest, under these conditions, passed a significant test.

Evidence that the compelling interests of government are not all powerful does not convince partisans of the value of government that works. Disagreeing with court rulings, partisans fixate on their claim that the US Constitution guarantees unlimited individual rights. This claim renders any compelling interest of the state into a burden. Partisans reject exposure to teaching and learning in traditional public education because exposure per se is tantamount to the abandonment of closely held partisanship priorities. For partisans, this is an intolerable burden.

In the same way, exposure to contemporary social reality (including compliance with the rule of law that aids and abets the navigation of the precarious-balance between individual rights and the government's interests in compelling the common good) is a burden rejected by partisans as a violation of their interpretation of the founding principles of government upon which the rule of law is based.

Partisans assert that it any compelling interest of government is a burden because government interests stand in the way of the exercise of absolutist partisan outcomes (e.g., universal singularity, one comprehensive doctrine). For partisans, the compelling interests of government are coercive because the purpose and practices of public education force parents/caregivers to abandon partisanship.

But compelling state interests are not ipso facto a burden, in part, because "no guarantee exists in the Constitution that subgroups will be supported and maintained" (Reich, 2002, p. 452). When the practices and policies of "government schools" do not prioritize the proclivities of partisan individuals and do not allow parental rights to supersede rights of "others," a burden exists only in the eyes of partisan beholders.

Government and its compelling interests do not constitute the only burden that partisans perceive lurking in traditional public education. The malign and intrusive presence of the outside-world throughout public schooling is a burden because this representation of contemporary social reality is not partisanship-centric.

THE OUTSIDE WORLD

Disconnecting students from threatening issues, topics, controversies, challenges, and difficult knowledge, partisans forestall the counterproductive influences of the outside world. After all, within the outside world are countless threats to what is right and what is true.

Putting students and their learning into the ideological box canyon of partisan education secures a future for these students anchored by static-balance. In the absence of the burdens created for partisanship by the influence of the outside world, closely held beliefs become learning.

Partisan education serves as a bulwark against the infiltration of this "real world" into the thinking, beliefs, decision-making, and behaviors of students. Serving as an individual's protective bubble, partisan education isolates pre-identified students from the malicious effects of being in the world. Excluding the outside world from education becomes a priority for those dedicated to the supremacy of closely held beliefs.

To thwart the existential threat presented by the outside world, a political action committee in Texas encouraged visitors on its website to report concerns and issues in a local school district such as "sexually inappropriate content in books or curricula; anti-bias training or diversity, equity, and inclusion work; social emotional learning; anti-American bias in instruction or teaching environment; and Critical Race Theory" (Richman and Smith, 2022, para. 8).

Controlling and restricting exposure to the outside world, partisan education prepares students to enact the ideal world of partisanship priorities. Eliminating the influences of the outside world in traditional public education by banning books and uncomfortable topics, burdens are lifted and partisanship narrows learning to ideological comfort zones.

One of these zones developed when the Indiana legislature approved a bill "that centers on what books students should and should not have access to in school. The final version of the legislation was largely decided behind closed doors" (Weddle, 2023, para. 1).

Partisanship Accommodations

The influence of the outside world, from a partisan's point of view, is pernicious. But, as discussion about the Amish and the Hasidic communities reveals, partisanship can coexist with the outside world and the compelling interests of government. Not all partisans are duty-bound to dismantle the public sector in the name of their closely held beliefs.

The Amish, alongside their honorable, court-validated efforts to sustain their ideal world, have accommodated the influence of the outside world.

McConnell and Hurst (2006) identify "increasing entanglement with the market economy" by the Amish (p. 237). Amish ways have adapted to developments in the outside world that further the Amish way of life.

For the Amish, the outside world is a source of *greater socioeconomic differentiation* (farming is no longer the predominant employment for Amish men), *increased purchasing power* (non-agricultural jobs provide higher incomes), and *specialized knowledge* (economic differentiation and greater purchasing power make it important to learn about technology, insurance, and legal issues) (McConnell and Hurst, 2006).

In response to these increasing points of contacts with the outside world that do not conflict with the closely held beliefs and practices of the community, some contemporary Amish pursue learning beyond eighth grade. For example, findings indicate that the Amish took advantage of a GED program offered by a county's adult education program. Some Amish enrolled in a variety of classes designed for adults to earn certifications in specialized or technical fields (McConnell and Hurst, 2006).

The Amish involved in this study proved to be avid consumers of newspapers and magazines in addition to patronizing the local library system's bookmobile. The researchers who conducted the study concluded that "it is clearly a mistake to equate the end of formal schooling with the end of learning in the Amish community" (McConnell and Hurst, 2006, p. 248).

If there is accommodation with the influence of the outside world in the Hasidic community, it is expressed as a willingness to accept government funding for special education services (Shapiro and Rosenthal, 2022). Nevertheless, the outside world continues to have little impact on or engagement from the students who attend and graduate from *yeshivas*.

Yeshiva students have little or no contact with learning that facilitates involvement with the outside world. This leaves them illiterate in English. Partisan education taken to this extreme means students are unable to function meaningfully in the outside world (Shapiro and Rosenthal, 2022).

DOWN A FEAR-FILLED RABBIT HOLE

Fear is a powerful emotion. Partisans wield this power to convince parents/caregivers that traditional public education is filled with danger.

Innuendos about the dangers in public schools and about the threats endemic to the outside world lead to conjecture and rumor which entail preemptive what-ifs about the fearful burdens of government schools on partisan priorities. Dangers and threats readily reverberate in the partisanship echo chamber and are symbolized by hypothetical what-ifs such as the following:

- What happens to my child when public education is a haven for learning that rejects closely held beliefs?
- What if public schools are a deliberate attempt to interfere with my rights as a parent/caregiver?
- What if public educators have malevolent designs for the students they serve?
- What if, as one gubernatorial candidate from Michigan told a Moms for Liberty chapter, "the COVID-19 vaccine [is] a 'genetic altering shot'" (Little, 2021, para. 5), and what if government intrusion like this is a constant part of what my child experiences in public school?

Questions, innuendos, myths, and stories render partisan conjecture and falsehood into fact. Fear guides the way down the many rabbit holes of partisanship: public education harms children, denies faith, abandons patriotism, favors "others," and fails "winners."

Mesmerized by fear, enraged by fear, empowered by fear, partisans actively transform traditional public education—a public thing that earns positive regard from more than 60 percent of US parents and caregivers (Phi Delta Kappa, nd)—into their own worst nightmare. Fearful parents and caregivers turn to partisanship because they are certain that fear-filled questions prove that traditional public education is the abject denial of what is right and what is true.

Fear convinces partisans that an alarming situation exists. Answering the alarm, the principles of faith and the tenets of ideology coalesce in what will be referred to for the remainder of this discussion as *partisan education*. Partisan education restores the certainties of boutique-ideology to US classrooms. Partisan control of teaching and learning eases fear because it replaces learning to navigate precarious-balance with the comfort zones of static-balance.

TO RESTORE PARTISANSHIP IN US EDUCATION

One way to explain the rationale for the contemporary attack on traditional public education is by realizing that partisans believe they lost control of America's schooling and, in the twenty-first century, are attempting to recapture it. Partisanship is emerging from its cocoon. Instead of remaining hidden—in the form of privatization- or choice-education (Swensson, 2023)—partisanship has taken wing.

The educational marketplace is the perfect ecosystem for this metamorphosis. Restoring the priorities of partisanship to teaching and learning is the task of individuals and entities convinced that their closely held beliefs merit re-integration into the day-to-day practices of public education where the outside world and unorthodox instruction now corrode patriotism, faith, parental rights, and what-to-think.

Following a script whose climax is the demise of traditional public education, partisans portray public schools as villains. The attack on public education features an ensemble cast of actors well positioned to undo the villainous intentions and nefarious purpose of public schools.

These "stars" of partisanship include preemptive censorship, universal singularity, and exclusive rights. Partisans assemble on stage to enact a performance that will be referred to here as *the revolt of the likeminded*.

Chapter 6

Revolt of the Likeminded

United by faith, by ideology, and by the belief that unlimited individual rights are sacrosanct under the US Constitution, parents/caregivers and other partisans foment the revolt of the likeminded.

The revolt of the likeminded is carried out as a function of ironclad allegiance to partisanship. Revolting, parents/caregivers and others demand "the freedom to reject what they perceive as a politically correct, assembly-line, one-size-fits-all approach to their children's education" (Klicka and Phillips, 1997, p. 81). Partisanship, the origin of and the sustenance for the revolt of the likeminded, is envisioned as the mainstay of America's future teaching and learning.

NO LIKEMINDED PARENT LEFT BEHIND

Foundationalism, evangelism, dominionism, free market theory—all guarantee that no likeminded parent/caregiver is left behind in the fight to control US education. The revolt of the likeminded is underway in the twenty-first century because partisans have reached several conclusions about the purpose and practices of traditional public education:

- Social-emotional learning is "another vehicle for anti-white racism" (Kingkade and Hixenbaugh, 2021, para. 18).
- Social-emotional learning is believed to have the potential for sexual grooming of students because it "teaches students to put their trust in educators over the instructions of their parents" (Kingkade and Hixenbaugh, 2021, para. 19).
- Lessons at the elementary school level that focus on emotions are seen as preparing "children for sex trafficking by teaching them to be accepting of LGBTQ identities and introducing them to books about sex, gender and sexuality" (Kingkade and Hixenbaugh, 2021, para. 8).

Family adults and other partisans revolt because they believe that traditional public education usurps parental authority over "aspects of upbringing [that] can be governed by the comprehensive doctrines and conceptions of the good" (Neufeld and Davis, 2010, p. 105). The revolt of the likeminded is directed at traditional public education for deviating from the comprehensive domains of families and the absolute rights of parents.

The upheaval meant to install partisan education is a revolt against unknowns and against uncertainty. The revolt of the likeminded is the intention to impose static-balance through ideological control over public education. Stability ensues when rigid patterns for teaching and learning yield the certainties of partisanship. The outcome of the revolt of the likeminded is the universal singularity that sustains a partisan social reality.

The revolt of the likeminded marches toward this social reality, for example, under the banners of discrimination and restriction found in Florida law, the statute often referenced as the Don't Say Gay Bill (Ravitch, 2022). The likeminded intend to eradicate thinking untethered to closely held beliefs and to foster exclusion found only in the educational marketplace.

Limiting the Universe of Discourse

A marketplace, by its nature, is limited. There's only so much space for so many vendors; only so much can be sold.

The revolt of the likeminded is an effort to conjoin education with the marketplace so that learning shrinks to a tiny realm of subjects, topics, and issues relevant for and integral to partisanship. The revolt of the likeminded is undertaken to install partisanship as educational royalty within this realm and to curtail teaching strategies and student meaning-making that do not rely upon closely held beliefs.

Shrinking the universe of discourse may seem like an impossible task. But the revolt of the likeminded has allies in state legislatures. To restrain what's available in US schools and to establish a viable educational marketplace, several states have passed what are referred to as *memory laws*.

These "laws are being used to ban a negative perception of a violent past, in this case America's history with slavery" (Conway, 2022, p. 715). Memory laws "are imposed 'to limit public debate on the national past by banning oppositional or minority views, in contrast to the principles of free speech and deliberative democracy'" (Conway, 2022, p. 715).

With this authoritative back-up, then, the revolt of the likeminded targets public schools because they do not conform, in the absence of legislative coercion, to the purposeful restrictions without which partisanship cannot function. The goal of the revolt of the likeminded is to establish partisan education as an ideological safe place isolated from the thought, debate, and unknowns that suffuse the outside world.

This goal ensures that students are guarded by the best interests of adult-centric education. Memory laws and other partisanship limitations are the building blocks of what-to-think.

What-to-think is the destination of partisan education. For students, learning what-to-think reinforces a structured worldview built from partisan expectations, theories, and dictates. Student thinking is not meant to diverge from these certainties. Insulating students from the universe of discourse relegates diversity, controversy, social issues, and a myriad of additional outside world conundrums to the status of "loser." The revolt of the likeminded is nothing less than censorship to guarantee the victory of closely held beliefs:

- In Virginia, proposed policy changes "would reverse current state protections for transgender students" (Jimenez, 2022, p. 6A). The implementation of these changes confronts rulings by Federal courts that the US Constitution and Title IX "protect transgender students from school bathroom policies that prohibit them from affirming their gender identity" (Jimenez, 2022, p. 6A).
- Partisan education, including free market mechanisms like charter schools, virtual schools, vouchers, and tax credits, prioritizes "better results at a cheaper cost to the taxpaying public" (Ali, 2019, p. 104). The meaning of "better" is galvanized to the preferences of adults and ideologues. "Better" is not a student-centric descriptor; there is little or no positive achievement difference when comparing student achievement in partisan education with student achievement in public education (Swensson, Ellis, and Shaffer, 2019a).

Rejecting How to Think and the Common Good

How to think, one segment of the purpose of public education, engages students with ideas that are rejected as inconvenient lessons in partisan education (Swensson, 2023). The other key element of the purpose of public schools, the common good, is irrelevant to partisans because the common good does not abandon "others." The purpose of traditional public education constitutes a threat to what-to-think and to exclusion.

Partisan education encumbers teaching and learning with principles of ideology and faith while partisans defame public educators for not doing so. But traditional public schools do not, and cannot, conform to the principles of any one ideology or faith.

Partisanship rejects such neutrality. The purpose of traditional public schools is rejected in favor of conformity with principles and practices espoused by family, houses of worship, or ideologically based entities.

Promoting the supremacy of individual rights as the baseline for society, partisanship prioritizes the destruction of a working balance between individual rights and the common good. When partisan education invests in unrestricted individual rights, the conjunction between compelling interests of government and individual rights is not for sale in the educational marketplace.

Partisanship allays ideological fears—of scarcity, of government overreach, of "others"—when unlimited individual rights replace the purpose of traditional public education. The revolt of the likeminded hides its intentions by coopting words like *transparency*, *liberty*, and *freedom*. Caught up in the frenzy of revolt, partisans do not promote participatory citizenship for government that works.

Rather, these parents/caregivers "likely feel as if they are simply parents (private individuals with specific concerns for their children) or fellow parents—a likeminded community looking out for the best interests of their children" (Stitzlein, 2015, p. 58).

This likeminded community detaches itself from non-partisans and the common good. After all, to act as a citizen pursuing the common good is tantamount to forsaking the primacy of singularity. Clinging to the role of "shopper," partisans treat education as a personal possession (Hinnefeld, 2023a).

Partisans are in the carnival-barker business when they claim that the revolt of the likeminded is a matter of *common sense* or *"Liberty"* or *parental rights*. If fine print accompanied all the partisan shouting, there would be a revelation—usually unnoticed by non-partisans—that partisanship promises schools that curtail rigorous academic challenges, censor classroom topics, and enforce narrow ideological expectations.

These promises offer partisans a choice of education that's best for their children without regard for what's best for all children. The revolt of the likeminded practices the art of the straw man to overwhelm policies, practices, and outcomes of traditional public education.

THE ART OF THE STRAW MAN

Setting up a straw man, a scapegoat, is simple. The art of the straw man lies in creating a target so malevolent, so threatening, so fear-inducing, *and* so fragile that knocking it down is both easy and ideologically satisfying. Artful straw men are intentionally offensive and enrage the sensibilities of partisans.

Partisans assemble straw men from the social reality and educational purpose embraced by non-partisans. Sowing fear and providing a vivid contrast between closely held beliefs and the dangers within traditional public education, straw men are often built from today's headlines. Partisans construct and knock down a variety of straw men including:

- "teaching and learning about race, policies and practices relating to LGBTQ student rights, [and] student access to books or social emotional learning" (Meckler, 2022, para. 4).
- schooling that provides "not only 'instruction' around gender identity and sexual orientation but also 'classroom discussion' of these topics" (Ravitch, 2022, para. 8).

Identifying straw men, likeminded revolutionaries assure each other that public education is a danger to the best interests of adults. Knocking down straw men reinforces the certainty that the best interests of adults are required to reform public education.

Convinced by the rectitude of their perspective, partisans could care less about a question which illustrates how the revolt of the likeminded is an assault on learning, *the public*, and constitutional democracy: "At what point does a minority in a school setting become enough to influence the practice of the majority" (Marshall, 2014, 142)?

ORTHODOXY TRUMPS MAJORITY RULE

Unwilling to countenance the concept of majority rule, partisans revolt on behalf of orthodoxy for education that is dedicated to the eradication of the rights of "others." When the likeminded revolt in the name of educational orthodoxy, "Liberty" is the right that partisans assign to themselves to knock down majority rule and impose minority rule.

"Liberty" claimed by partisans sets up "others" as a straw man. After all, non-partisans cannot be trusted with "Liberty" for two reasons. First, "Liberty" is assigned only to the likeminded and constitutes permission to revolt. Non-partisans are granted no such permission.

Second, the revolt of the likeminded overturns majority rule. Universal singularity signals the efficiency of minority rule. Minority rule is necessary and sufficient if partisans are to reform public education by exercising the right to deny the closely held beliefs of "others." "Others" who insist on majority rule are knocked down and replaced by "Liberty" that functions as the imposition of minority (partisan) rule.

Educational orthodoxy fuels the revolt of the likeminded and supplies meaning to "Liberty" as a staple of partisanship. However, conveyed in the comments of one observer, "Liberty" inherits its own contradiction because "the parents (fighting to ban books) are saying we should have a right to determine what our children can read and what our kids can access on the shelf, but how can you say I deny the right to *another* parent who says my child *does* need this book" (emphasis original) (Willen, 2022, para. 7). The likeminded are revolting to control curriculum, truncate teaching, and limit learning. Knocking down straw men along the way is an important maintenance activity that keeps the revolt running smoothly.

The extent to which partisanship-as-orthodoxy in the twenty-first century has become a strident ideological perspective in the battle over US education is suggested by Conway who observes that,

> populist backlash movements whose *raison d'etre* is to normalize human hierarch [are involved] in an attempt to stall unification of the American people around the democratic principles of equality, realism, and commitment that would dismantle structural racial inequality and systemic inequity. (2022, p. 711)

Once the straw men fall, the likeminded install orthodoxy for education that is prejudice in favor of:

- Isolating students from public education.
- Manipulating the practices of public education to "protect" students from public education.
- Attacking public educators as the source of despicable behaviors.
- Maligning public educators and school board members as purveyors of child abuse (Little, 2021, para. 2).

One observer depicted the revolt of the likeminded as a circumstance in which "a relatively small group of hostile parents and community members are leading the charge, thwarting the wishes of the majority of parents and others who want kids to have an accurate, inclusive and skills-building education" (Rubin, 2022, para. 5).

The malign influence of *how to think* about the topics confronted by intellectual autonomy in public schools are, for the likeminded, threats to static-balance.

The structural divide between traditional public education and education for ideology is a significant obstacle to the future of democracy and to the nature of learning. The inability to grant a common or public good and the assertion of rights that deny the value of the common good for others are revolutionary barricades from which proponents of partisan education will not climb down.

Once fear about public education is invoked, *deus ex machina* is called upon to strengthen the script written to assure success for the revolt of the likeminded.

PART II

Deus Ex Machina in the Script for Partisanship

Chapter 7

Preemptive Censorship

In the firm belief that parental rights, ideological principles, and faith-based imperatives are ignored, defied, or countermanded by traditional public education, the likeminded take center stage and activate extraordinary powers they claim for themselves to forestall the purpose and practices of public schools.

At center stage, partisans call upon *deus ex machina* to end the villainy of public schools. At the forefront of the extraordinary interventions used to alter the script for US education is *preemptive censorship* (Hartsfield and Kimmel, 2020).

Preemptive censorship denies access to learning when partisans deem, in advance of their purchase or use, that teaching materials, books, instructional strategies, topics for classroom discussion, and/or library materials are harmful.

Deployed to prevent the purchase of books for libraries and classrooms, for example, preemption is employed to eliminate literature offensive to the closely held principles of partisanship and, as a result, are decried as "immoral," "pornographic," or "age-inappropriate."

Legislation in several states threatens school and public librarians with imprisonment and hefty fines if "harmful" books are available to children. In Arkansas, for example, "school and public librarians, as well as teachers, can be imprisoned for up to six years or fined $10,000 if they distribute obscene or harmful texts" (Natanson, 2023b, para. 4).

Observers indicate that such legislation creates a climate of fear that grows when many of these laws are vague about what constitutes "harmful" or "obscene" material. Educators note that the tidal wave of legislation seeking to remove books "will make sure the only literature students are exposed to fits into a narrow scope of what some people want the world to look like" (Natanson, 2023b, para. 7).

Proactive outrage preempts proscribed literature and captures what partisans consider to be moral high ground. Acting in the name of their moral high ground, partisans imply that public educators are intentionally prurient. Certain that preemption protects what is right and what is true, partisans stymie intellectual autonomy.

In pursuit of preemption, partisans confronted one Indiana school board screaming about book placements (Slaby, 2021). At a different school board meeting in the Hoosier State, a citizen was arrested during a book protest when his concealed handgun fell to the floor during the meeting (Slaby, 2021).

Elsewhere, in Texas, a state legislator listed 850 books that should be banned, and the governor of the state took book banning a step further by "insisting that education officials must investigate 'criminal activity in our public schools involving the availability of pornography'" (Willen, 2022, para. 11). In mid-2023, nationwide, "book bans were imposed in 138 school districts in 32 states, affecting nearly 4 million students in more than 5,000 schools" (Dvorak, 2023, para. 21).

Preemption of reading materials is the tip of the exclusionary iceberg. Legislative preemption is *deus ex machina* that excludes instructional practices, discussion topics, and "uncomfortable" ideas that represent *how to think*.

OH WHERE, OH WHERE HAS THINKING GONE?

Legislatures across the nation write *deus ex machina* into the script for schooling to curtail the right of students to receive communicated speech in classrooms about certain topics and issues. The freedoms guaranteed by the First Amendment to the US Constitution (i.e., the establishment clause and the free expression clause) are curtailed when partisan legislators limit the intentions of the curriculum and the content of instruction.

In several states, proposed legislation seeks to "limit what schools can teach, how they can interact with students, and allow parents to sue schools for violating provisions of the bill" (Herron and Beck, 2022, p. 12A).

Wisconsin state legislators "proposed legislation that would outlaw social emotional learning and other educational concepts that they labeled as 'state-sanctioned racism'" (Kingkade and Hixenbaugh, 2021, para. 13). A political action committee formed by Utah Parents United lobbied the state legislature successfully for "a bill banning 'sensitive materials' in schools, including books that could be viewed as 'pornographic or indecent'" (Harris and Alter, 2022, para. 15).

Across the United States, during 2022, state legislators "introduced at least 137 bills seeking to restrict teaching on topics such as race, gender, LGBTQ issues and American history" (Mervosh, 2022, para. 8). Quashing the freedom to learn, partisans call down *deus ex machina* to manipulate teaching and learning and to impose the "free expression" of closely held beliefs.

Manipulating thinking by "others," these extraordinary measures obliterate impediments to the rights claimed by partisanship that infest public schools. Teaching and learning become, thereby, a script featuring only words and scenes validated by partisanship.

One of the partisan founders of a group called Florida Citizens Alliance confirms that preemption and *deus ex machina* are useful, adult-centric, partisanship tools: "This is not about banning books, it's about protecting the innocence of our children and letting the parents decide what the child gets rather than having government schools indoctrinate our kids" (Harris and Alter, 2022, para. 6).

Discriminatory Thinking, Anyone?

Deus ex machina allows partisans to take aim at *how to think* represented in some of the most rigorous high school courses in the nation. State policies and administrative action in Florida, for instance, forbade all high schools from offering the Advanced Placement African American history course (McGraw, 2023, para. 7).

Teaching and learning in Advanced Placement courses incorporate open-ended learning activities including debate, discussion, investigation, research, and the exploration of difficult knowledge. The action taken by Florida, and similarly restrictive bills passed by legislatures in other states, ensures that the confines of partisanship thinking are the curriculum and censorship is the instruction.

The revolt of the likeminded, aided and abetted by *deus ex machina*, descends upon those elected to govern traditional public schools. "Outrage over pedagogy—mixed with parent frustration over Covid school closings and resistance to mandatory masking—turned public meetings of school boards across the nation into eruptive events of chanting, screaming [and] threats" (Bergner, 2022, para. 5).

A devotee of partisanship, the executive director of Patriot Mobile Action (a Texas cell phone company that provides funding to ideologically aligned candidates for local school boards) took a "stand against school anti-racism initiatives, which she and her supporters have argued indoctrinate children with anti-white and anti-American views" (Hixenbaugh, 2022, para. 13).

WHAT IF PREEMPTION DOESN'T WORK?

Decades of economic transformation, the relentless march of technology into daily life, changing demographic and cultural influences, legislative and judicial protection for equity, compelling interests of government, and the effects of globalization—all, and more, are elements in the social reality of the twenty-first century that contradict and threaten the priorities of partisanship.

Many of these factors and forces represent change in US society and exert influence throughout public education. Although preemption and legislation often turn the tide against the insidious effects of public education, partisans fear the staying power of the outside world.

If *deus ex machina* doesn't bring the script of public education into compliance with principles of ideology and tenets of faith, then partisans turn to *anarchic dissent*.

Chapter 8

Anarchic Dissent

Responding to the fears that undergird partisanship, and enforcing the outcomes that serve the best interests of partisans, *anarchic dissent* acts out the intentions of the likeminded to demolish traditional public education.

Anarchic dissent is comprised of outward and visible extraordinary measures enacted to bring to fruition the inward and closely held social reality postulated at the baseline of partisan education. Anarchic dissent is reinforced by human tendencies and self-aggrandizing behaviors including *default choice, the Stroop test, my-side bias* (Molden and Higgins, 2012), and *synergy of struggle* (Granger, 2008).

Default choice is the human tendency, as Mezirow puts it, "to reject ideas that fail to fit our preconceptions labeling those ideas as unworthy of consideration—aberrations, nonsense, irrelevant, weird or mistaken" (1997, p. 5). In addition, humans tend to adhere to simple, easily understood ideas that lend themselves to automatic responses. This tendency is referred to as the Stroop test (Ludwig, 2022).

My-side bias "is the human tendency to justify choices simply because they are self-serving" (Swensson, 2023, p. 20). Synergy of struggle rewards the proponents of a perspective with the experience of "emotional depth as well as the intellectual satisfaction that springs from the transformation of uncertainty, ambivalence, and complexity into an understandable phenomenon" (Edelman, 1988, p. 40, quoted in Granger, 2008, p. 212).

In combination, these tendencies are tailor-made to draw adherents to partisanship and, at the same time, reinforce partisans in the belief that their principles, beliefs, and ideologies constitute what is right and what is true.

These self-affirming tendencies reinforce the purpose and value of anarchic dissent, the behaviors that stoke the partisan blast furnace of certainty. Ideological certainty serves as the rebar in the concrete of what-to-think. Anarchic dissent is self-satisfying, self-rationalizing action generated when partisans internalize, then apply, what-to-think. Certainty is promoted when anarchic dissent assails traditional public education.

ANARCHIC DISSENT IS AS PARTISANSHIP DOES

Partisanship is adherence to closely held beliefs. For the likeminded, these beliefs deserve to be the baseline for social reality in the twenty-first century. Leveraging cost-avoidance, fear, universal singularity, and the other tenets of partisanship, the likeminded pursue legislation, manufacture social media, and generate outrage to inspire anarchic dissent and create this reality. Anarchic dissent pushes partisanship priorities into public education which means that, for partisans, public schools are the entryway to the social transformation envisioned by the likeminded.

Partisans relish the impact of anarchic dissent and accelerate its effects using *Gish Gallop*, a strategy usually reserved for formal debates. Gish Gallop, in formal debate, is the release of so many arguments, accusations, falsehoods, irrelevant data, myths, unrelated statements, and innuendos that any coherent defense is impossible. Echoing this strategy, partisans send a stampede of invective, legislation, accusation, protest, and recrimination to trample traditional public education and its proponents.

Gish Gallop is applied to convince parents and caregivers that ominous characteristics of public education are so omnipresent that what families value most in life, their children, face certain danger in public schools. Claims that these dangers are endemic and deliberate motivate partisans to adopt anarchic dissent as the means to deconstruct traditional public education and, thus, save their children.

The Ideological Foundation of Anarchic Dissent

Ideology and faith amalgamated within partisanship inspire the assault on traditional public education. Driven by human tendencies and advanced through the behaviors of anarchic dissent, this amalgamation is "a form of false consciousness which distorts one's perceptions of social reality and serves the interests of the dominant class in a society" (Apple, 2004, pp. 18–19, quoted in Brantmeier, 2007, p. 1).

Partisans perceive that contemporary social reality has invaded public school classrooms and constitutes a threat to the dominance that partisanship deserves. Contemporary social reality poses a danger, then, to likeminded members of the younger generation whose informal education is rooted in partisan priorities.

So dire is the threat posed by contemporary social reality that anarchic dissent is called upon to control US education. Activated by the consciousness unique to partisanship, anarchic dissent functions as a wrecking ball:

- Created, in part, to oppose COVID-19 vaccines and mask mandates, a local Indiana group "believes that 'anti-American ideologies' are infiltrating schools and communities at large and want to work towards combating that" (Beck, 2022, para. 1).
- A national group, Free to Learn Action, shares information about school board candidates at the local level including whether individuals running for school board are registered as Republican or Democrat. Without pausing to acknowledge irony, this group asserts that their version of a quality K-12 education ensures that students are "free from 'pressure or requirements to subscribe to a singular worldview and activist curriculum with a political agenda'" (Beck, 2022, para. 1).
- Another national group, Moms for Liberty, indicates "they are 'dedicated to fighting for the survival of America by unifying, educating and empowering parents to defend their parental rights at all levels of government'" (Beck, 2022, para. 1). A cofounder of Moms for Liberty indicated that the group's respect for fundamental parental rights "is a catch-all for any [school board] candidate that does not want to 'co-parent with the government'" (Mansfield and Jimenez, 2022, para. 10).
- Purple for Parents of Indiana indicts public schools for "pushing out 'social justice agendas'" and for teaching critical race theory "under the guise of social emotional programs and diversity, equity and inclusion work" (Beck, 2022, para. 1).
- Parents Defending Education, another national organization, is "a group of 'corporate school privatizers going hard right to attack school boards, superintendents, principals, and teachers'" (Little, 2021, para. 1). The organization's website highlights public school districts whose practices or policies are thought to malign or neglect parental rights.
- Moms for Liberty in Florida took umbrage at a document for administrators in Brevard County that shared LGBTQ guidelines. These guidelines called attention to "the rights of students as delineated in state and federal laws, including the right to dress and use bathrooms according to the gender they identify with" (Jenkins, 2021, para. 3). In response to the guidelines, protesters besieged school board meetings chanting "Shame" when students, who identified as LGBTQ, attempted to speak. Other partisans who could not fit in the meeting room pounded on windows and doors (Jenkins, 2021).

If, as the old saying goes, perception is reality, then anarchic dissent is a response to the partisan perception that contemporary teaching and learning are frightening and dangerous.

PUBLIC DISSONANCE

Public dissonance is disharmony that lingers throughout the social structure of traditional public education in the wake of anarchic dissent. Public dissonance reverberates and rattles both public schooling and the social reality at the base of America's contemporary public sector.

Public dissonance is the sustained turbulence left in the wake of anarchic dissent. The demise of public education accelerates when unrelenting turbulence shakes the purpose and practices of public schools.

Public dissonance agitates the function of traditional public schools. Looking over their shoulders, public educators respond to dissonance that lingers in the wake of partisan legislation. Lingering, public dissonance keeps public educators off balance when:

- "Personal, stinging accusations [claim] that school board members don't understand or care about students, families, or the communities where they live" (Golden, 2021, para. 3).
- Digital ads are posted that claim "children are being 'held captive' by schools. One ad—posted by a school board candidate in Maryland supported by the 1776 Project PAC—shows a picture of stacked books bearing the words 'equity,' 'grooming,' 'indoctrination' and 'critical race theory'" (Binkley and Carr-Smyth, 2022, para. 14).
- The Florida Department of Education launches an investigation of a fifth-grade teacher who showed her students a Disney film as part of unit on the environment. The investigation started because one parent complained about a gay character in this animated film (Rosales and Garcia, 2023).

Day-to-day turbulence is showered upon public schools (e.g., standardized testing results, test prep instruction, insufficient funding, staffing shortages, acrimonious social media posts) that gives partisans leverage to advocate for the demolition of public schools in the name of the best interests of adults.

Turbulence upends public school governance and prioritizes adult-centric outcomes without regard for and in contravention of the best interests of students. Turbulence, fueled by the ideological prioritization of competition, sorts out adult winners (e.g., partisan schools) and student losers (e.g., pupils in underfunded public schools).

The greater the turbulence generated to highlight the malfeasance of public education and public educators, the greater the likelihood that the likeminded rally around anarchic dissent. Public dissonance calls attention to the necessity to rectify the unorthodox nature of public education and install educational practices grounded by what is right and what is true. Public dissonance reminds partisans to initiate the circumstances most conducive to the right that leads to universal singularity: *freedom from* government.

Public Dissonance on Behalf of Parental Rights

Public dissonance lingers after anarchic dissent is employed as a battering ram to shatter the purpose and practices of traditional public education. Under these conditions, individuals jettison their role as citizens and forswear meaningful participation in representative democracy.

Public dissonance rattles teaching and learning in public schools. Public dissonance is the persistent turbulence that calls attention to public schools as nothing less than government interference with the right of partisans to impose what-to-think. Rather than improve public schools, partisans ramp up turbulence.

Turbulence and anarchic dissent in the name of partisanship have shaken teaching and learning in public schools for decades. For instance, in the mid-1970s, when a school district in West Virginia approved the purchase of textbooks accused of multiculturalism and atheism, chaos ensued. "As a result, 'homes were firebombed, schools were dynamited, [and] gunfire was exchanged'" (Salzman, 2022, p. 1073).

Critics of traditional public schools justify long-standing opposition to traditional public education and applaud, for example, that "the Home School Legal Defense Association has been fighting since 1983 to protect the right of parents to direct the education and training of their children" (Klicka and Phillips, 1997, p. 81).

Allies of this association condemned "'family abuse' by the child protective services industry, as well as a growing feeling that parents have been disenfranchised from the education of their children by 'experts' and heavy-handed bureaucrats" (Klicka and Phillips, 1997, p. 81).

Thrown off balance by public dissonance, public educators and their allies struggle to ignore turbulence, turn away from public dissonance, and respond to Gish Gallop. Confronting this onslaught is time-consuming and enervating. At times, public educators take their eye off the prize of student-centric education.

For example, lingering dissonance and the mere implication that anarchic dissent might ensue led an Alabama school district to cancel elementary school appearances by an award-winning Black author. School district officials indicated that one parent complained about the content in the social media presence of the author. In response to the complaint, the school district canceled the author's visits with school children (Wu, 2023).

Anarchic dissent and public dissonance roil the purpose and daily practice of traditional public education; this intentional crisis in public schools is a partisan remodeling project dedicated to demolishing teaching and learning in traditional public education. Anarchic dissent is the equivalent of an ideological "demo day" when the sledgehammers of partisanship swing into public education.

ANARCHIC DISSENT: IDEOLOGICAL "DEMO DAY"

School districts, school board members, and public educators insist that traditional public education is wedded neither to political nor ideological agendas. Evidence, data, and endorsements from members of the school community demonstrate that traditional public education is a focus on learning. This focus is dedicated to the premise that all US students deserve opportunities to acquire the capabilities to make up their own minds within the context of the nation's constitutional democracy.

Traditional public education embraces the social reality of US society as it evolves within the framework established by the rule of law and the common good.

Undeterred by evidence, disdainful of the common good, and enraged by government intrusion, adherents of free market theory initiated the first call for demo day in the middle of the twentieth century (Friedman, 1955).

Events, publications, and policies amplified this call and reinforced the partisan rationale for demolishing public schooling. Reasoning that traditional public education embraced a social reality detrimental to singularity and opposed to closely held beliefs, parents, caregivers, ideologues, legislators, and citizens reacted to key developments in US history that symbolized the need for ideological sledge hammers:

- Passage of the National Defense Education Act (1958);
- *Brown v. Board* (1954); and
- *A Nation at Risk* (National Commission on Excellence in Education, 1983).

Additional court rulings, research-based instructional strategies, and social trends antithetical to closely held beliefs reinforced the partisan conviction that traditional public education was irredeemable. The deficiencies embedded in traditional public education made demo day a partisan priority. Primed for demo day, partisans grab several sledgehammers.

A Six-Pound Partisan Sledgehammer

Hammering away, those with closely held religious beliefs responded to the National Defense Education Act (1958). This legislation (in part, a frenzied reaction to the launch of Sputnik by the Soviet Union) focused on improving instruction and resources for teaching math and science in public schools. It also facilitated funding for textbooks that taught evolution. Striking a blow against this government intrusion in education, partisans proceeded from the conviction that that they were *in the world, but not of the world* (Bindewald, 2015): "In other words they believed that they were heavenly creatures living in a sinful world, and they felt an eminent need to engage with mainstream culture to steer it in, what was from their perspective, a more godly direction" (Manatt, 1995, quoted in Bindewald, 2015, p. 98).

Positioning traditional public education as a citadel of disbelief, partisans enact demo day guided by the tenets of faith that are not of the world. Anarchic dissent, in this way, brings US education back into line with faith-centered principles. Often in the name of faith-based principles, the primal scream of ideologues is a call for anarchic dissent (Bindewald, 2015) and the demolition of public education.

A Twelve-Pound Partisan Sledgehammer

Partisans are certain that government has no right to impinge on the nation's promises which, as partisanship would have it, guarantee unfettered individual liberty. Proponents of partisan education are certain that overreach, intrusion, indoctrination, and interference are woven within the purpose and practices of traditional public education because public schools are government entities.

Anarchic dissent is not merely raucous disruption of school board meetings and personal confrontation with public educators. Swinging this second sledgehammer means that partisans pound away at democracy to clear the way for charter schools governed by unelected groups of individuals (Beck, 2023). Legislation establishes this retreat from participatory citizenship and facilitates partisan disdain for "others" who are unworthy of charter school enrollment.

Sometimes referenced as a board of directors or as a charter board, charter school governance is not directly accountable to families of students enrolled in the charter. Moreover, these directors and charter boards are not accountable to the community from which they receive funding (i.e., vouchers, tax credit scholarships).

Silencing the participatory citizenship of parents/caregivers and denying fiscal accountability to taxpayers, unelected boards of partisan schools are the ultimate expression of universal singularity. Disconnected from voters and obligated only to their own best interests, boards of most charter schools act on behalf of cherished marketplace priorities.

When charter school governance no longer serves as a small piece of democracy, these schools symbolize the voice of ideology prejudiced in favor of adult-centric education. This denial of democracy censors voices of the community and abandons accountability traditionally associated with the public sector.

The Granddaddy of All Partisan Sledgehammers

The most damaging sledgehammer of all subsumes public school governance in the ethos of partisanship on behalf of success for the revolt of the like-minded. Smashing the purpose and practices of traditional public education, partisans swing the sledgehammer of dog-eat-dog competition into school board elections.

Beginning in the 1900s, local school board elections across the US have been non-partisan. Historically, the political affiliation of a school board candidate was not the "calling card" that voters pay attention to when casting their ballot.

Partisans are eager, however, to reverse this trend and to label school board candidates with the name and priorities of one political party or another (Binkley and Carr Smyth, 2022; Herron, 2022). Such a label has the power to affirm, or deny, a candidate's alignment with the closely held imperatives of partisanship. Instead of focusing on how a potential school board member will enhance the student-centric character of a school district, partisan identification of school board candidates maximizes a focus on ideological priorities.

When partisans reorient the non-partisan nature of school board elections, the platform or priority of a political party becomes the impetus behind this sledgehammer (Herron, 2022). Swinging away in the name of a political party, candidates who choose the priorities of partisanship approach school governance as their personal remodeling project.

The force behind this sledgehammer and the resulting demolition of traditional public education explains "the fervor to elect conservative school board members nationwide under the guise of reforming the public education system" (Conway, 2022, p. 714).

Local school board elections, a small piece of democracy and participatory citizenship, offer foes of traditional public education a prime opportunity to bring ideology and faith into public school classrooms. Static-balance is weaponized by citizens who use the structure of democracy to impugn

K-12 public education for any number of faults including teaching critical race theory (Terruso and Hanna, 2021).

Partisan candidates who want to oust non-partisan members on a board of education mince no words about the foundation for their candidacy. One candidate wrote that she wanted "to get back to the basics of teaching academics [and] stop wasting their education on [social-emotional learning, critical race theory, and] politics" (Herron and Beck, 2022, p. 12A).

When formerly non-partisan and student-centric elections become combat zones where anarchic dissent and public dissonance hold sway, local school board contests are transformed into magnets for ideological dollars. For instance, partisans harvest dark money from 1776 Action and additional support from Tea Party adherents who include representatives of the Koch empire (Sollenberger, 2021).

One long-time donor to political causes in Pennsylvania contributed five hundred thousand dollars to various school board candidates during election campaigns in 2021 (Terruso and Hanna, 2021). Political action committees and individual ideologues contribute to candidates whose intentions for school board governance prioritize the principles and tenets of partisanship (Kurtzleben, 2022).

The impact of this third sledgehammer is a devastating blow to traditional public education. Partisanship is funded to replace the purpose of public education with the supremacy of individual rights at the root of a false consciousness:

- In Texas, the political action committee known as Prosper Citizen Group vowed to support candidates for school board who "believe in individual liberty, limited government, transparency and accountability, fiscal responsibility, and alignment to the U.S. and Texas Constitution" (Richman and Smith, 2022, para. 8).
- In Florida, Moms for Liberty fund candidates who "respect fundamental parental rights" and who are unwilling to "co-parent with the government" (Mansfield and Jimenez, 2022, para. 41).
- Nationwide, sizable sums of money are spent by political action committees to support "candidates who promise to scale back teachings on race and sexuality, remove offending books from libraries and nix plans for gender neutral bathrooms or transgender-inclusive sports teams" (Binkley and Carr-Smyth, 2022, para. 3).

THE ANARCHIC DISSONANCE OF "LIBERTY"

When partisanship is integral to education and becomes the centerpiece of social reality, partisans refer to this result as "Liberty." "Liberty" is the implementation of closely held beliefs that assigns robust and unlimited individual rights to partisans. When partisans invoke "Liberty," they speak to the guarantee of their own rights and their own freedom. "Liberty" is not available to "others."

Anarchic dissent and public dissonance help build this distorted social consciousness. Partisans embrace distortion and transform liberty, as it is generally perceived, into "Liberty," an image altered as if it's reflected in a funhouse mirror. When partisans intentionally clash with the purpose of traditional public education, the disassociation with contemporary social reality is sufficient to implode the common meaning of liberty.

When it comes to partisan education, "the liberty at issue is not just the parental right to choose a child's school, but also the individual liberty interest of the child to be free from state-prescribed orthodoxy in terms of what to learn and how to think" (Tang, 2018, p. 353).

Boutique-ideology is the foundation for this false consciousness. Upending social reality and driving a wedge into the structure of public education, partisans employ consumer relations to indict non-partisan priorities (e.g., compelling interests of government, the common good, working government) as the abrogation of "Liberty."

Partisans erect "Liberty" as a barrier against inclusive public school enrollment practices, against programs designed to support and grow the capabilities of "others," and against learning untethered from the orthodox certainties of partisan education. Distance and separation from contemporary social reality and commonly accepted definitions for foundational vocabulary constitute the public dissonance effects of "Liberty."

The common understanding of liberty, on the other hand, sustains the purpose of public education and empowers instruction that engages students with the universe of discourse. Lost in partisan demands for parental rights, abandoned when partisans achieve "Liberty," and denied by the educational marketplace, are components of liberty as this term is understood in its foundational role in constitutional democracy:

1. Government has purposes and these purposes constitute compelling interests in some policies, statutes, or actions. The legitimate, compelling purposes of government require participatory citizenship facilitated through education that permits "people to develop the tools necessary

to meaningfully participate in representative democracy" (Imoukhuede, 2019, p. 457).
2. No right exists for one ideological cohort to supersede the rights of any other cohort within the public sector. The spaces of the public sector, like public education, exist for the common good without preference for, or privilege of, ideological spaces that conflict with the common good.

SAVING PUBLIC EDUCATION BY DESTROYING IT

Reform is a code word used by partisans to obscure the intentions of demo day and the wreckage it creates. Reform for public education, as partisans employ it, resembles a statement attributed to an Army officer during the Vietnam War: *It became necessary to destroy the town in order to save it* (Arnett, 1968, p. 14). In this echo of a tragic observation, the ethos of partisanship is revealed: saving schooling in America can only be accomplished by destroying public education.

Although it can be argued that envisioning destruction as a primary outcome of partisanship is hyperbolic, the partisanship fixation on winning and its destructive consequences is not a secret. Reform signals partisans, and public educators, that contemporary public schools are worthless and require a complete overhaul.

The effort to destroy public education to save US education has had a significant impact. Researchers report that the "'virulent stream of hyperpartisan political conflict' has had 'a chilling effect on high school education'" (Edsall, 2022, para. 31; Rubin, 2022, para. 2).

The extent of this chilling effect and the destruction wrought on learning by reform is symbolized in legislation passed in Arizona that walls off teaching and learning by prohibiting public educators from engaging students with instruction or a course in which "an individual . . . is inherently racist, sexist, or oppressive, whether consciously or unconsciously" (Salzman, 2022, p. 1072).

Destruction does not represent, however, the first intention of those who proposed reform for traditional public education. At first, reform signaled the intention to improve, not destroy, public schools. Several improvement goals illuminate this first instinct about the purpose of educational reform:

1. To ignite competition between schools that would lead to substantial improvement because "bad schools" would see decreasing enrollment and go out of business.
2. To give all parents/caregivers the chance to choose a school that better met the needs of their child(ren).

3. To foster a climate of innovation that curtailed or ended the bureaucratic achievement desert for learning known as traditional public schools (Schneider, 2019, para. 7–9).

Promises about the purpose of reform are one thing. The outcomes of reform in the twenty-first century are another:

- "'Charter school innovation has often been in areas like new uses of funding and governance,' rather than in instructional designs" (Schneider, 2019, para. 12).
- Mechanisms (i.e., vouchers, charter schools, tax credit scholarships) created to deliver partisan education and its purpose "*necessarily* involve the redirection of state aid from public to private schools and increase the number of children enrolled in private schools where society's shared values may not be taught" (Tang, 2018, p. 360).
- "A study by researchers at the University of Notre Dame found Indiana students using vouchers were not benefitting, but instead falling behind academically" (Lubienski, 2023, para. 4).
- "Families have faced challenges in navigating a marketplace of choices . . . [while] . . . charter networks can spend millions of dollars on advertising campaigns" (Schneider, 2019, para. 13).
- A voucher program proposed in Tennessee "would siphon off over $7,500 per student—or over $375 million in the first five years—from funds appropriated by the General Assembly to maintain and support the Metro Nashville Public Schools (MNPS) and Shelby County (Memphis) Schools" (Public Funds Public Schools, 2020, para. 3).
- "Backed by a surge of campaign spending from far-right Christian megadonors, Republicans in Texas and nationwide are pushing legislation that would siphon money from public education under the banner of 'parents' rights'" (Hixenbaugh, 2023, para. 3).
- Privatization reform allows free market schools to "discriminate against students on the basis of religion, LGBTQ status, disability, income level, and other required characteristics" (Public Funds Public Schools, 2020, para. 8).

Reform is the *bait* used to encourage families who otherwise might not participate in partisan education. Results are the *switch*. The partisan Gish Gallop unloaded on the public not only buries attention to the disparity between partisan promises and results but also prioritizes winning because destruction of traditional public education is the primary objective of reform.

The self-aggrandizing promises of partisanship are powerful incentives for partisans to abandon improvement and engage in destruction.

Lost when this onslaught turns reform into a winner-take-all ethos are the purpose of public education, knowing along with others, and equity. US schooling, amid the ruins of public education intended by partisanship, arrives at its destination: *partisan education*, which will be discussed shortly.

Chapter 9

Rights and US Education

Throughout US history, rights are framed in two ways: *negative* rights or *positive* rights. *Freedom from* government action is the frame for a negative right. Conversely, the *obligation of* government to act is the frame for a positive right (Imoukhuede, 2019).

Traditional public education is the result of the *obligation of* government to act. This obligation puts intellectual autonomy, derived in part from knowing along with others, at the forefront of student capabilities for participatory citizenship. Participatory citizenship is the facility to navigate precarious-balance between individual rights and the compelling interests of government. In the nation's constitutional democracy, navigating precarious-balance permits the government to act on behalf of the common good.

Framed as a negative right, partisan education is the result of *freedom from* government action. Closely held beliefs, *deus ex machina*, anarchic dissent, and public dissonance are employed to attenuate partisan education from government action.

Freedom from government action, ironically, is often a product of legislation. Such enabling legislation locks in the distance between partisan schooling and government. Partisanship is a source of the structural split in education. Divided, US education embraces the value of static-balance as a remedy for the dangers that lurk on the other side of the split in traditional public schools.

Disconnected from government intrusion and freed from entanglements with contemporary social reality, partisan education acquires status as an ideologically secure zone. In this case, unlimited individual rights endow partisans with the freedom to impose closely held beliefs in schooling as they see fit.

With this review of rights and their frames as a backdrop, no right to public education framed one way or the other exists within the US Constitution. Public education is, however, "recognized by each state in the United States of America as a right" (Imoukhuede, 2019, p. 443).

Eighteen state constitutions direct state government to create and maintain merely a *general system* of free public schools. Ten other states are obligated to establish an *efficient* or *thorough and efficient* system of public education, while fifteen additional states are directed by their constitutions to establish a *uniform system* for public education (Hartman, 2005).

State legislatures are given the responsibility for enacting each constitution's directive about public schooling. Thus, at least in the wording of state constitutions, public education is framed as the *obligation of* government to act. *How* government acts to fulfill this obligation, however, varies from state to state.

THE EXCLUSIVE RIGHTS OF PARTISANSHIP

Framed as *freedom from* government action, partisan education portends a social reality in which universal singularity and unlimited individual rights abandon the common good. *Freedom from* government action is first among the unlimited individual rights claimed by partisans *as if* partisanship is the exclusive arbiter of social reality.

Selecting from the cornucopia of rights granted to themselves, partisans double down on individual singularity as a mandatory outcome of US schooling. Universal singularity is a fulsome disconnection from government, and as a self-serving partisan construct, is its own frame for the attenuations from the public sector and government fostered through partisan education.

In the absence of governmental obligation, partisans impose on education to enact universal singularity in the sense that government-free teaching and learning inculcates closely held beliefs. "Liberty" is invoked as the outcome of partisan education that permits partisans to exclude and restrict "others."

The certainty that unlimited individual rights are required to fend off any *obligation of* government to act is the freedom that partisans pursue down innumerable rabbit holes. Each rabbit hole is a comfort zone dedicated to the rights prioritized throughout partisanship including:

- The right to perpetual winning.
- The right to determine losers.
- The right to impose what-to-think.

THE RIGHT TO PERPETUAL WINNING

Partisanship and competition are ideological soulmates (Swensson and Shaffer, 2020). Competition perpetuates winning for those who deserve it.

Partisans, the deserving few, (1) have exclusive access and motivation to follow the rules of competition (i.e., principles and tenets of ideology and faith encapsulated in free market theory), and (2) employ these rules as the right to declare themselves winners when partisanship is inflicted on US education.

Self-proclaimed and self-perpetuating winning is the right partisans claim when principles of ideology and faith leverage closely held beliefs to control schooling. The right to perpetual winning is galvanized to the certainty that competition favors partisans. Circular reasoning like this, reinforced by my-side bias and the synergy of struggle, justifies the educational decisions and actions of partisans.

The educational marketplace is enamored of competition because perpetual winning means perpetual losing by "others." Marketplace competition ensures that both winners and losers are predetermined. This partisans-take-all ethos undermines traditional public education as "a commitment to democracy and the citizens who compose it" (Stitzlein, 2020, p. 369).

Standardized Testing: Brass Knuckles in Partisan Boxing Gloves

Enforcing and maximizing competition to guarantee winning, partisans design and impose standardized testing throughout public education. Standardized testing, a winner-take-all enterprise, is educationally reliable competition in the same way that a boxing match is a fair contest when one fighter hides brass knuckles in the boxing gloves.

Celebrated by partisans as a meaningful benchmark for educational quality, standardized testing is little more than a numbers template dropped on top of students and schools in support of separating winners from losers (Swensson, Ellis, and Shaffer, 2019b).

The false consciousness that underlies standardized testing (Swensson, 2023) is that test score accountability is the same as excellence in teaching and learning. This fiasco masquerading as fair competition forces public schools to weave and duck in a vain attempt to avoid being knocked out by contraband-laden boxing gloves (Swensson, Ellis, and Shaffer, 2019b).

Standardized testing is designed to confine learning and referee the rules assigned to public education by partisanship. Partisan education, schools privileged with gerrymandered funding, and/or schools in high-wealth communities, are hands-down favorites to win under these conditions. The "fix" is in when some partisan schools are not required to administer standardized tests.

THE RIGHT TO DETERMINE LOSERS

Just as perpetual winning is a non-negotiable right assigned by partisans to themselves, losing is a right assigned by partisanship to non-partisans. Competition—the intentional winnowing of those unworthy to participate in the marketplace—is an ideological weapon.

Those who seek the demise of public schools and victory for partisan consciousness in education use competition to fend off panic when closely held beliefs and principles are not winners in local schools, in school governance, or in legislative decision-making. Under these conditions, fear motivates partisans to decree preemption via testing competition.

Failure to get your way, after all, is the same as losing for partisans. Or, more to the point of partisanship, the fear of losing is the fear of "others" winning.

"Others" are entities or individuals intentionally excluded from partisanship. Advocates for public education are designated as "others" because non-compliance with the principles, tenets, and tactics of partisanship consigns public educators to the losers' bracket. "Others" are destined to lose not only because they fail to conform to closely held beliefs but also because they are trapped in the Catch-22 fashioned in the preemptive nexus between insufficient funding and learning success judged by test scores.

So entrenched is losing as a function of partisan education that free market schools (e.g., charter schools, virtual schools) are expected to lose when, for a variety of reasons, these mechanisms cease to operate and close. Partisans tout such failures as an indicator of marketplace efficiency; a properly functioning marketplace eliminates "inefficient" schools.

Going out of business, losing, is the outcome if partisan schools lose enrollment and funding. In the adult-centric marketplace, these developments are emblematic of failure to adhere to the closely held beliefs that guarantee marketplace success.

Partisans often fail to acknowledge that "inefficiency" or other missteps in the marketplace do not account for all the partisan schools that lose. When partisan schools go out of business it can be the result of administrative malfeasance, fraud, or never opening for business in the first place (Swensson, Lehman, and Ellis, 2021).

When a choice school goes out of business, enrolled students, their families, staff members, and the school community go from winning to losing. When partisan schools cease to operate, sometimes with little or no warning, students and their families are jettisoned from schools they chose. The irony associated with losing in the marketplace is that traditional public schools are waiting in the wings to support students who are tossed to the curb.

More to the point of the damage done by prioritizing survival of the fittest, partisan education has no regrets when students tossed out of an inefficient partisan school have no choice but to attend a public school already decimated by fiscal gerrymandering and ravaged by test score accountability. Ready to serve the students abandoned by partisanship are schools predestined to be marketplace losers.

As noted earlier in this discussion, partisanship principles predetermine enrollment choices made by partisan schools. "Educational choice" is little more than a consumer relations gambit that obscures the partisanship penchant for and commitment to exclusion. Choice schools are schools dedicated to the victory of partisanship principles. Students are disposable, subject to the whims of the marketplace.

It turns out that choice education is *freedom from* obligation to all students. The marketplace is *freedom from* obligation to the common good. These characteristics of choice education signify *freedom from* government. *Freedom from* government is the choice-of-choices made by partisans when "Liberty" is defined as the rightful advantage of those invested in partisanship.

The Right to Defund Losers

Losing, of course, is expected, even encouraged, in the marketplace. Defunding traditional public schools (e.g., siphoning off funding, underfunding, educational gerrymandering) is a right that partisans exercise to ensure that there are losing schools.

But defunding is not only a matter of insufficient and inadequate funding for public schools. Defunding also entails removing *how to think* from teaching and learning with the result that students are denied opportunities for open futures. Defunding, in this sense, is preemption that undercuts the social reality most harmful to partisanship.

Social reality conducive to partisanship identifies cohorts of students as "losers." "Loser" students are presumed to lack the capabilities, life experiences, opportunities, race, and/or economic status that make them capable of "winning" in partisan education. These students' lives and futures are defunded; partisanship preempts resources so that these "losers" have no chance of survival in the boxing ring of marketplace competition (Swensson, Ellis, and Shaffer, 2019a).

This unethical and discriminatory determination denies the outcomes and opportunities that could result for students if partisanship did not predesignate their status.

It bears emphasizing that public educators, also, are designated as losers. Defunding occurs when marketplace principles facilitate legislative decisions that deny adequate compensation for public educators (Swensson, Lehman, and Ellis, 2021).

Weekly salaries for public educators have not kept pace with the weekly salaries of college graduates in other fields. Data from 2021 indicates that teachers made 32.9 percent less in weekly earnings than graduates in other fields (Edsall, 2022, para. 10). Analysts report this means that "wages are essentially unchanged from 2000 to 2020 after adjusting for inflation" (Edsall, 2022, para. 8).

This marketplace phenomenon, an indicator of low cost as a partisan priority, and an element in the destruction of public schooling, plays a role in the decreasing numbers of individuals who want to become public educators. "According to the National Center for Education Statistics, the number of students graduating from college with bachelor's degrees in education fell from 176,307 in 1970–71 to 104,008 in 2010–11 to 85,058 in 2019–20" (Edsall, 2022, para. 9).

Amid these manipulations that predesignate losers, public educators *are* relatively abundant in school districts that can support reasonable compensation. But defunding manufactured through legislation (i.e., educational gerrymandering) leads to fewer college-prepared public educators vying for positions in low-pay districts (Black, 2019).

Defunding emerges as just one more instance of competition designed to limit winning to those who deserve it. Fiscal hocus pocus, academic misdirection (e.g., standardized testing), instructional manipulation—all defund the full complement of educational resources with the potential to reach and improve the lives of all US students.

In the name of partisanship, efficiency, low-cost, preemption, restriction, and denial guarantee the staying power of the rights claimed for partisan education. Abundant predetermined and exclusive winning and the calculated defunding of losers confirm that the marketplace is amoral (Lubienski, 2013).

THE RIGHT TO WHAT-TO-THINK

What-to-think is the outcome of learning undertaken in thrall to the principles and tenets of partisanship. Partisan education erects what-to-think as the cognitive guardrails that prevent students from driving away from this destination and into the danger zone of the universe of discourse.

What-to-think is a partisan talisman used by some parents and caregivers to ward off fear of the unrestrained practices and unorthodox outcomes of public education. What-to-think is conjured up from the partisan comfort zones of competition, faith-centered tenets, exclusion of "others," singularity, reduced government, and low cost.

Students are cocooned in what-to-think, learning in and for a world bounded by the social reality favored by partisans. Mechanisms protect what-to-think so that partisan education is designed to perpetuate the effects of the marketplace. If partisans have any concerns about the fact that students taught what-to-think are just as likely to "lose" as to "win," few such doubts are evident as marketplace amorality, competition, and exclusion of "others" remain partisanship precepts in the twenty-first century.

What-to-think, consequently, is a right assumed by partisan education to limit student futures and the promises of democracy. When what-to-think restricts student capabilities, the nation's future (i.e., economic progress, political civility, participatory citizenship) is limited. Partisan education becomes the springboard for thinking that validates exclusionary citizenship. These unlimited individual rights are consigned to a few with the result that partisanship supersedes the compelling interest of government in the common good. What-to-think is a harbinger of partisan supremacy.

What-to-think empowers decision-making necessary and sufficient for partisan control over the rights of "others" and the practices of traditional public education. The right to what-to-think sustains static-balance in the destination that is partisan education.

The Right to Dumb Down Learning

Standardized testing sets the leading edge of restricted learning and establishes the right to dumb down learning. Defunding magnifies the effect of this right when students in low-wealth communities receive low test scores and, as a result, are condemned to test prep instruction. Instruction devoted to test prep is a frantic push for efficiency that further dumbs down learning.

Partisan insistence on efficiency and accountability as hallmarks of education becomes an encounter with the right to dumb down learning when standardized testing leads to the manipulation of instruction. Students, after beginning a new school year and a new grade level, are in place to learn the requirements for a new standardized test. But students can be designated as "losers" once the results of last year's standardized test are available.

Under these conditions, "losers" must return to standards and expectations from the previous year. This cycle condemns "losers" to *boomerang education*. Boomerang education is a hodgepodge of instructional strategies meant to engage "losers" with standards that come back from the previous school year to overlap with standards in the new school year. Students subjected to boomerang education over several years may account for test performance that is resistant to improvement.

Compounding the damage done by this retrograde learning experience, students required to improve their test scores from the previous year often are ineligible to take classes designated as "frills" (e.g., performing arts, vocational education, foreign language) or classes designated as higher level (e.g., Advanced Placement, International Baccalaureate).

Retrograde learning also means that students, whether designated as winners or losers by testing, are victimized by the right to dumb down learning. All students lose when educators are expected to adhere either to test prep priorities or to instructional pablum cooked up by partisanship restrictions on classroom topics, ideas, or issues.

What-to-think and dumbed down learning are rights that satisfy the adult-centric ethos of partisanship. Censoring and restricting classroom learning while boomeranging instruction for some students, proponents of partisanship determine what's best by looking in the mirror of ideological certainty.

A CIRCULAR BILL OF RIGHTS: PARTISANSHIP'S GIFT TO EDUCATION

Partisanship stacks the deck, gifting US education with a circular bill of rights. Proponents of partisan education interconnect their rights:

- What-to-think puts partisan education in position to (1) limit teaching and learning to prevent any departure from the principles of partisanship, and (2) nurture future partisans with the capabilities required to perpetuate the marketplace.
- What-to-think dumbs down instruction and facilitates the limitations embedded in partisan education. Imposing what-to-think on US classrooms is tantamount to stifling inquiry, curtailing research, eliminating authentic learning, forbidding engagement with the universe of discourse, and forestalling investigation into unknowns. Closely held beliefs, thus, are immunized against intellectual autonomy.
- Circling as if this motion is the same as moving forward, partisanship assumes the right to control US education with efficiencies such as standardized testing.
- In the same way that partisanship assumes the right to impose competition tailored to the ideological imperatives of the free market, educational choice is the right assigned to winners. Educational choice embodies the principles and processes through which partisan schooling selects winners. Consumer relations pretend that winners select partisan education. But partisan education preordains winners to best meet the needs of parents/caregivers who choose partisanship and to sustain the rights partisans claim for themselves.

- The vortex created by these rights is an intentionally destructive force. Preemption and exclusion swirl through traditional public education tossing aside students, ideas, and futures deemed antithetical to boutique-ideology. The cyclonic effect of the rights of partisanship represents the persistent and calamitous impact of anarchic dissent and public dissonance.

Competition in the marketplace ensures that only losers need to worry about scarcity; partisan education puts the bounteous rights of partisanship into the hands of winners (Chubb and Moe, 1990; Friedman, 1955). Winner-take-all is the ultimate right found in the Circular Bill of Rights. The right to win in the marketplace is the truth that unlimited individual rights apply when the interests of partisans supersede characteristics of the outside world.

PART III

The Foes of Traditional Public Education

Chapter 10

Partisan Education

Partisan education is teaching and learning aligned with principles of ideology and tenets of faith redolent with anti-government bias, exclusionary citizenship, self-proclaimed superiority, parental rights, and certainty. Partisan education is the choice to place students in the embrace of schooling for universal singularity. Partisan education replaces conscience with survival of the fittest.

The purpose of partisan education is ideological, beginning with the immutable determinants of free market theory. From this foundation, partisan education advances the closely held beliefs of parents/caregivers who "want the sole discretion to direct their children's education, beyond just choosing between public and private schools" (Solochek, 2021, para. 10).

MORE TO IDEOLOGY THAN MEETS THE EYE

A dictionary definition tells us that ideology is "the ideas and manner of thinking characteristic of a group, social class, or individual" (*New Oxford American Dictionary*). This definition provides a preliminary insight into the foundation of partisan education.

But the ideas and manner of thinking offered as partisan education adhere to a more transactional definition of ideology: "A social construction that serves the interests of a situated group of people within a society; unequal power relationships are maintained through the propagation of an ideology" (Brantmeier, 2007, pp. 2–3).

Partisan education is grounded in transactional relationships that prioritize the social construction necessary to (1) assign partisanship to the apex of social reality and (2) guarantee separation from the common good. These transactional relationships entail teaching and learning that perpetuate self-validating, self-perpetuating, and absolutist outcomes.

From these relationships, partisanship derives a collectivist unity of purpose. This collectivist mindset gives no quarter to any perspective beyond the boundaries set by partisanship. The situated group of ideologues striving to implement partisan education invests in both anarchic dissent and public dissonance to sustain the ideological restrictions that enforce these boundaries.

For partisans, there is unity in separation represented by the collectivist mindset embodied in the ideological outcomes of transactional relationships. The effects of partisanship and the goals of partisanship are shared across otherwise unaffiliated partisans and partisan entities in the sense that they emerge from, and maintain, universal singularity.

PARTISAN EDUCATION: A TRANSACTIONAL RELATIONSHIP

Stitzlein (2020) observes that school-choice parents and guardians have a transactional relationship with public things like traditional public education. The transactional relationship that is partisan education, as this discussion indicates, is a one-way interaction: *what's in it for me?*

Interactions rooted in universal singularity, these transactional relationships assign no value to *the public* and express scant regard for "others." These relationships focus on one-upmanship and focus on the expectation that a collectivist mindset leads to winning. Winning, in transactional terms, requires partisans to ensure that relationships, especially those in the public sector, are exclusionary.

Radical departures from the primary purpose of traditional public education, partisan transactional relationships reject knowing along with others.

Transactional Relationships Are Exclusionary

Transactional relationships that articulate partisanship exclude "others," those who are designated losers. The transactional relationships chosen by proponents of partisan education invoke an acquisitive approach to interactions that can be distilled as *what's mine is mine and what's yours is worthless unless it's mine*. Teaching and learning in partisan education are constructed from the templates of rigid patterns of thought designed to nourish the collectivist mindset.

These patterns of thought focus exclusively on what's best for the ends, goals, and objectives of partisanship. When these patterns are applied to a limited range of topics and issues, exclusion triumphs and adult-centric education takes hold. Partisan education and transactional relationships exclude the outside world and contemporary social reality.

Transactional relationships evince an adherence to tenets of faith, dedication to ideological principles, and facilitation of the amorality of the marketplace. Transactional relationships that sustain partisanship are guided by the certainties granted by faith represented in evangelism, dominionism, and fundamentalism. As Bindewald observes,

> rather than educating for autonomy—equipping children with the tools that they will need to be able to pursue their own goals in life, to think critically so that they might be able to evaluate multiple conceptions of the good, or to be able to navigate the increasingly complex and globalized world—fundamentalists are most concerned with preserving and promoting their traditional faith. (2015, p. 106)

Rigid patterns of thought and behavior facilitate exclusion and reflect the self-aggrandizement that partisans exercise during transactional relationships. Transactional relationships uphold the social reality of partisanship as an absolutist, all-or-nothing-at-all proposition.

But threatening this proposition is an outcome of traditional public education destined to shatter rigid patterns of thought: *intellectual autonomy*.

A Pox on the House of Intellectual Autonomy

Unwilling to be dislodged from the certainties of closely held beliefs, partisans distance themselves from the uncertainties in the outside world and claim the right to annex traditional public education to the collectivist mindset.

Partisans cling tenaciously to the self-validations, self-serving principles, and beliefs with which they surround themselves. Partisan education constitutes the educational comfort zone where partisanship can flourish. Partisans intend to superimpose this comfort zone on traditional public education via legislation and anarchic dissent.

But this battle plan is vulnerable.

Intellectual autonomy is an outcome of learning in public education. Intellectual autonomy is a significant impediment to transactional relationships; *how-to-think* does not rely on rigid patterns of thought designed to eventuate in a collectivist mindset. In the first place, intellectual autonomy threatens what-to-think because it represents knowing along with others.

What's more, intellectual autonomy is a threat to the collectivist mindset because it fosters concerns for others as the common good. The common good is variable, reciprocal, and evolving. A collectivist mindset, on the other hand, is the destination where partisans take cover beside the certainty of static-balance.

Thinking that facilitates the common good empowers participatory citizenship. Participatory citizenship corrodes the penchant of partisans for knowing *without* others. Partisanship is vulnerable when citizens have the capacities to prefer and sustain government that works.

The vulnerability of partisanship is exacerbated when knowing along with others, the common good, and participatory citizenship become pillars of social reality in which no protected class or cohort is privileged with either exclusionary rights or exclusionary education. Intellectual autonomy batters the premise that universal singularity suffices when pluralism is the core of constitutional democracy.

Ideological principles and tenets of faith, certainly, are part of social reality in contemporary America but they are not the determinants that define social reality. It's the human quest, and public education's quest, for learning that yields open futures fulfilled by intellectual autonomy that defines contemporary social reality. Knowing along with others, intellectual autonomy, open futures, and the principles and practices that foster the common good—all threaten the fragile social structure envisioned by weakly connected partisans.

Fundamentally, partisanship's answer to intellectual autonomy is retrenchment. Hunkering down in an effort to protect closely held beliefs from the purpose of public education and taking a step backward to restore a lost presence in public school, partisans are afraid. Faced with multiple threats, partisans rally on behalf of static-balance.

Fear, then, is utilized as a partisanship repair kit. Fear of loss of primacy and fear of "others" accessing resources and rights motivate partisans to restore schooling that doubles down on the imposition of comprehensive doctrine, fills the gaps in the armor of certainty, and confirms the viability of universal singularity.

Fear permits partisan rage against rational, elite, public educators and the practices in public schools that engage students with capabilities that undermine certainty. To win, partisans require both schooling and social reality to reflect marketplace amorality.

The amorality of the marketplace prioritizes losers who are denied access to scarce partisan-centric rights. Social consciousness under these circumstances is the understanding that winning is a scarce commodity and that the rights that ensure winning are due to partisans only (Lee, 2018).

Fear ensues when intellectual autonomy and open futures portend access to winning by multitudes of "others" who learn from the purpose and practices of traditional public education. Fear ensues when the common good replaces universal singularity. The common good does not prioritize self-aggrandizement for a cohort of self-selected recipients.

To guarantee winning and to strengthen the armor provided by the closely held beliefs of partisanship, partisan education rejects knowing along with others, the universe of discourse, and respectful engagement among and between those with differing views. "If fundamentalists do not guard against children learning to think on their own, they risk turning out adults who will choose a path inharmonious or even opposed to their own" (Bindewald, 2015, 107).

THE ETHOS OF PARTISAN EDUCATION

Simply put, partisan education is an expression of the characteristic spirit of those dedicated "to remake the public schools in their own image" (Reich, 2002, 448).

Partisan education manifests the spirit of the community of the likeminded. Partisan education is made in the image of prejudice in favor of partisanship. More circular reasoning depicts the heart of partisans' penchant for self-justification, supported by ironclad allegiance to self-aggrandizement. Self-serving justification is a partisan staple in the effort to safeguard, and expand, partisan education.

Partisanship will never surrender to scarcity. Marshalling scarce resources and rights to maximize denial to "others," the point of safeguarding closely held beliefs is to ensure they are abundant for those who claim them.

The antipathy directed toward intellectual autonomy, the common good, equity, *how to think*, and learning along with others is testimony to partisan fear that the attributes of traditional public education and the capabilities of public school students are threats to abundant personal possession.

Rationing scarce rights and resources, partisan education does not permit profligate, pointless access to its ideological treasures by non-partisans. To ensure exclusive access to these ideological jewels, partisans direct anarchic dissent at public schools to stymie purpose and practices that have the potential to unravel partisanship and its priorities.

The ethos of partisan education forms a bulwark against the unorthodox misdirection of public education. To stop the counterproductive, wasteful practices of public schooling, transactional relationships embrace personal economics for winning through so-called choice education.

For instance, mechanisms are choices in a marketplace that permit partisans to make less-cost-and-more-for-me economic decisions. The amorality of the marketplace ensures that partisans can make these decisions but non-partisans cannot. Legislation encourages personal economic choices for schooling by reducing the burdens of taxation and/or school tuition. Self-aggrandizement is front and center under these conditions when scarce ideological benefits are doled out to those who deserve them.

Theoretically, partisans might warm to traditional public education if public schools were perceived as the equivalent of a cash-back credit card. After all, citizenship education equips students with capabilities to exercise rights "owed to others," and these capabilities are provided to all students. No exclusive cohort of individuals is the sole beneficiary of citizenship rights when reciprocity and precarious-balance on behalf of the common good are taught to all.

However, "all" and the common good are serious problems because they symbolize ignorance of exclusivity and the denial of the dangers of scarcity. Partisanship is an intentional flight from the "criterion of reciprocity" which "requires that citizens offer terms of social cooperation—specifically, principles of justice for their society's basic structure—that they think other citizens might reasonably accept" (Neufeld and Davis, 2010, p. 96). Social cooperation, for partisans, is the antithesis of competition. The amoral marketplace evinces, as discussed earlier, the educational destination where only partisans may win.

For partisans, the inevitable and all-encompassing marketplace becomes the ultimate transactional relationship in which closely held beliefs interact with self-chosen rights in favor of supremacy of the individual which entails the right to ensure that scarcity is a burden reserved for "others."

This is a social reality in which partisan education, like personal economic decisions, exists in service to singularity. The dividends that partisans expect from learning cannot be separated from the belief that there is no value in learning to accommodate precarious-balance as a feature of the social structure that depends on both social cooperation and the reasonable acceptance of this social structure among and by "others."

Defined as "exclusion of *the public* and the prioritization of selected individuals" (Swensson, 2023, p. 11), singularity eradicates the common good. The right to singularity appropriated by partisans ensures that transactional relationships proceed from the premise that both winners and losers deserve their fates. For the proponents of partisan education and free market theory, singularity is the apotheosis of "Liberty."

Stipulated for this discussion, *universal singularity* is unlimited "Liberty," engendered by the pursuit of closely held beliefs, to disconnect from contemporary social reality and to impose the exclusive rights of partisanship on the outside world. Partisan education succeeds when winners are separated from losers; universal singularity perpetuates competition and exclusion. Universal singularity separates learning from participatory citizenship.

Thus, "Liberty" is the permission partisans give to themselves to separate and divide the social structure. "Liberty" is necessary and sufficient for the efficiency of transactional relationships that produce universal singularity. Separating partisans from non-partisans is a personal-economics outcome of the adult-centric competition over the distribution of resources. From the rigid patterns of thought and behavior that drive partisanship as a collectivist mindset come the all-or-nothing-at-all ethos of "Liberty."

"Liberty" is a product of the ideological and faith-centered baseline of partisanship. "Liberty" is utilized as the justification for the sledgehammers of partisanship that break apart social cooperation in favor of unlimited individual rights and unlimited denial of these rights to "others." Ideological freedom is carte blanche taken by partisans to impose a mindset upon those individuals unwilling to submit to this belief system.

Partisan education, intentionally disconnected from the social reality of the outside world, encases students, learning, and futures in "Liberty," an ideological and faith-centered amber.

PARTISAN EDUCATION: WHAT IS RIGHT AND WHAT IS TRUE

Partisan education is designed to further a consciousness congruent with the ethos of partisanship that posits what is right and what is true. Static-balance is foisted upon public education and democracy when what is right and what is true are defined solely through the ethos of partisanship.

Partisan education separates teaching and learning from the universe of discourse and the wide range of ideas, perspectives, and insights that populate this universe. Learning offered in partisan education, instead, entails limited perspectives, restricted beliefs, and singularity. These intentions and outcomes are shaped by a template for what is right and what is true: orthodoxy for education.

ORTHODOXY: LIMITLESS OR LIMITED?

Neufeld and Davis (2010) point out that most of the internal life of families is given special priority by the basic structure of society in a constitutional democracy. This priority is a freedom that grants "considerable scope to families to organize their internal life in a variety of different ways, as dictated by their respective comprehensive doctrines and conceptions of the good" (Neufeld and Davis, 2010, p. 102).

The special priority given to the internal life of families balances in constitutional democracy so that,

> For an institution to be considered part of the basic structure, it must be one that reasonable persons would recognize as playing a *necessary* role in their

society's system of fair social cooperation, that is, an institution necessary for satisfying the criterion of reciprocity in their public social relations with each other. (Neufeld and Davis, 2010, p. 106)

But the considerable scope freely given to organize the internal life of a family is twisted beyond recognition when partisans exert "Liberty" upon society. Partisans claim "Liberty" as their right to remodel social reality with absolutist comprehensive doctrines and conceptions of the good that contradict reciprocal public social relations with the internal life of non-partisan families. Variety, diversity, and differences, in this way, are not recognized as part of the basic structure of US society.

Failing to acknowledge society's system of fair social cooperation, partisans deny that families are obliged to satisfy reciprocity in their public social relations. Claiming the right to subordinate all institutions to that of the family, partisans upend the basic structure of society in the name of "Liberty." Unlimited individual rights allow partisans to construct certainty.

Tilted away from reciprocity and the common good, partisanship envisions a social reality constructed, paradoxically, from disconnections. Disconnection, exclusion, and separation constitute the infrastructure of universal singularity.

As a basic part of social reality from a partisan's point of view, universal singularity means, among other things, that there is no necessity for families to satisfy the interests of non-partisans for the common good. Partisanship eschews any criterion of reciprocity relevant to participatory citizenship and denies any relationship with rights claimed by non-partisans.

Reciprocity is pointless in the transactional relationships that fuel partisanship and reciprocity is irrelevant in the exercise of education for orthodoxy.

Partisanship, in this regard, postulates that there is no difference between a family's right to organize their internal life and the family's right to impress this "internal life" on the lives of those outside the (partisanship) family. For partisans, there is no boundary between a family's internal power for organization in accordance with partisanship and its right to exert this power as what is best for the outside world.

Certainty that universal singularity is owed to partisans undermines the basic structure of contemporary society. Reciprocity, concerns for others, and agreement about the nature of fair social cooperation play no role in the construction of the basic structure of partisan social reality.

WEAPONIZING PARTISAN EDUCATION

Partisanship retreats from the public sector and the common good. Fleeing toward their destination, partisans weaponize education to defeat the unorthodox practices and purpose of traditional public education.

Partisan education is weaponized to confront ideas and practices that contradict closely held beliefs. The purpose of public education and its connectedness (e.g., knowing along with others on behalf of the common good; reciprocity) are threats to the collectivist internal life espoused through partisanship.

Perhaps invoking the adage that the best offense is a good defense, partisans weaponize their right to impose closely held beliefs. Of greatest value in this regard is moving away from traditional education to learning as a fortress mentality. A fortress unto itself, surrounded by immutable truths and self-assigned rights, partisan education:

- Weaponizes distance to separate students from the universe of discourse.
- Weaponizes competition because losers and winners are distinct ideological cohorts and social structure is built efficiently when losers are at the "bottom" and winners are at the "top."
- Weaponizes transactional relationships to separate learning from the social reality of twenty-first-century America and traditional public education.

A RETREAT FROM CONSCIENCE

Weaponized, partisanship institutionalizes a *retreat from conscience*. Stitzlein points out that *conscience* "is the direct descendant and exact cognate of the Latin *conscientia*, which is the word for knowledge, *scientia*, to which is added the prefix with. Thus, it means to know along with others" (Stevens, 1984, p. 171, quoted in Stitzlein, 2015, p. 64)

Knowing along with others is fundamental to the purpose of traditional public education. Traditional public education fosters knowing along with others, in part, to ensure that the purpose of public schooling is impervious to "the influence of parents who teach their children that their way is the only good and right way to live, which presumes that the conscience of others is of less value" (Wenneborg, 2020, p. 46).

For partisans, knowing along with others raises the specter of engaging with ideas and concepts unrelated to or disassociated from faith and ideology. Abandoning "uncomfortable" topics, restricting the scope of academic disciplines (e.g., science, social studies), penalizing public educators who engage students with *how to think*, and maximizing separation, partisan education retreats from conscience.

Knowing along with others, from the perspective of partisanship, is a losing enterprise. Winners, of course, are those endowed with closely held beliefs which, by their very nature, cannot tolerate knowing along with "others." Not only is knowing along with others antithetical to universal singularity but any enactment of empathy, or a consciousness about others and their learning, threatens winning.

Likeminded legislation emboldens the retreat from conscience:

- New Hampshire's legislature passed HB 542 that requires public schools to offer an alternative as "'an exception to specific course material based on a parents' or legal guardian's determination that the material is objectionable' (New Hampshire HB 542)" (Stitzlein, 2015, 64).
- "As of April 1, 2022, forty-two states had introduced bills or taken other steps to regulate the discussion of race in public schools" (Salzman, 2022, 1071).
- Texas statutes forbid teachers and school leaders from incorporating in any course the idea that "with respect to their relationship to American values, slavery and racism are anything other than deviations from . . . the authentic founding principles of the United States" (Salzman, 2022, pp. 1071–72).
- An Idaho legislator proposed legislation that meant "all Idaho school districts would have to allow parents to withdraw their children from any activity, class or program that the parents believe 'impairs the parents' firmly held beliefs, values or principles'" (Russell, 2015, para. 1).

Instead of knowing along with others, partisan education is knowing (1) universal singularity, (2) retreat from conscience, and (3) separation. When partisan education retreats from conscience, "others" are separated from learning, intellectual autonomy collapses, participatory citizenship atrophies, and constitutional democracy is at risk.

COMMITMENT TO PREEMPTION

Partisan networks join the retreat from conscience to further separate learners from the practices and outcomes of traditional public schools. For example, the Council for National Policy "has designs to educate children outside of public schools in order to reorient education toward Christian nationalism and transform the culture of the nation" (Cunningham, 2022, para. 1).

The retreat from conscience weaponizes what-to-think. What-to-think is an example of foundationalism which is described as justifying any educational proposition via *basic principles*. "These basic principles or beliefs have to be self-evident, which means that they do not require any further justification" (Scott, 2014, p. 18). When learning is about principles that are self-evident, *how to think*, intellectual autonomy, and open futures are preempted.

Tenets of faith and principles of ideology are unquestioned, basic, and self-evident from the perspective of partisans. What-to-think—framed by limitation, restriction, and censorship—is the blueprint for learning that requires no justification. What-to-think fosters conformity so that intellect, creativity, and behavior retreat from the universe of discourse toward a destination given the seal of partisanship approval.

What-to-think is education construed as a destination, not a journey (Swensson and Shaffer, 2020). This destination is tailor made to "filter out the complex and competing views that students need to face to become informed and active citizens who understand the array of beliefs and conflicts in the world around them" (Stitzlein, 2015, p. 65).

However, foundationalism, and the other faith-centric initiatives within partisan education, are not only about self-evident, *destinational* learning.

Seeking to eradicate the purpose and practice of public education in the twenty-first century, the proponents of partisan education preempt "others" by endorsing (1) segregation academies (Shaffer and Dincher, 2020), (2) limitation of topics/issues eligible for classroom discussion (Edsall, 2022), and (3) state funding for privatization education where enrollment practices bar attendance by preempted cohorts of students (Swensson, Ellis, and Shaffer, 2019a).

Universal singularity and the aspiration to preemption, in combination, give partisan education the equivalent of a non-stick ideological coating: preselected "losers" are prohibited from learning along with partisans by the tactics, principles, fears, and tenets that comprise the ethos of partisan education.

"Others" are not welcome in the marketplace, preempted because they are not worthy of, and constitute competition for, the scarce resources reserved for partisans. Partisan education promotes *learning without others*. To this end, what-to-think reinforces the effects of the retreat from conscience and justifies the disconnections that nurture universal singularity.

The retreat from conscience is brutally consistent with the transactional relationships of partisanship. Learning *without* others is the individualized separation in a closed worldview consistent with the social reality favored through partisanship. Partisan education does not and will not pursue intellectual autonomy, emancipatory education, or knowing along with others. The retreat from knowing along with others protects learners in partisan education from damage to, or refutation of, closely held beliefs.

Further, the retreat facilitated by what-to-think endows winners with the capabilities required to avoid or ignore meaning-making about the outside world. Partisan education liberates students when they are separated from the complications and complexities inherent in engagement with and/or navigation of precarious-balance in the universe of discourse.

This degree of separation removes students from the effects of teaching and learning in public schools. Damage to closely held beliefs is avoided because partisan education shields students from thinking that accommodates precarious-balance in the universe of discourse where "there are no fixed truths or totally definitive knowledge, and because circumstances change, the human condition may be best understood as a continuous effort to negotiate contested meanings" (Mezirow, 2000, p. 3, quoted in Hoggan and Kloubert, 2020, p. 300).

Retreating Is "Winning"

Anarchic dissent and the retreat from conscience combine during the assault on traditional public education. Fifty percent of public school principals responding to a survey indicated that parents/caregivers or citizens "sought to limit or challenge teaching and learning about issues of race and racism" while "nearly half report challenges to school policies and practices related to LGBTQ student rights" (Rubin, 2022, para. 3).

Scholars confirm that "emotions in response to these issues have run high within communities, resulting in the harassment of educators, bans against literature depicting diverse characters, and calls for increased parental involvement in deciding academic content" (Edsall, 2022, para. 19). Weaponizing the retreat from conscience, partisans, again, proclaim disconnection, separation, and singularity as "Liberty" that permits and affirms the right of any parent to impose family expectations on traditional public education and non-partisans.

Money: The Partisanship Weapon for Choice

Money is a weapon cherished by partisans because winning an election can be expensive. With partisans actively engaged in school board elections, funding becomes essential for victory. School governance, it turns out, is susceptible to marketplace manipulations. School board election is for sale and the cost of victory can be paid by political action committees (PACs) (Binkley and Carr Smith, 2022; Richman and Smith, 2022).

Before the twenty-first century, PACs rarely had a direct connection with or impact upon school board elections (Terruso and Hanna, 2021). Infiltrating partisanship into these contests, however, the foes of traditional public education transformed school board elections into contests that determine survival of the financially fittest.

Squaring off, PACs have been created to fund school board candidates who either (1) support the imposition of partisan education or (2) defend traditional public education.

PACs speak to communities about disparate priorities for school governance. Sharing views and perceptions online or through other public forums, PACs rally parents/caregivers and citizens to join the conflict over the purpose and outcomes of US education.

For example, Defend Texas Liberty is a PAC that draws most of its funding from "a pair of billionaire oil and fracking magnates who've expressed the view that government and education should be guided by biblical values" (Hixenbaugh, 2023, para. 2).

PACs have proliferated, especially in suburban locations (Rubin, 2022). For instance, "at least 10 conservative PACs have launched in the past year in cities across the Dallas area with the goal of steering local districts in a more conservative direction" (Richman and Smith, 2022, para. 3).

PACs in Indiana represent the tenor and intensity of the opposing perspectives battling over school governance:

- *Indiana Family Action PAC:* A significant issue for this PAC is "supporting parental rights in schools" and continuing "to fight for your right to raise your children as you see fit" (Beck, 2022, para. 1).
- *Indiana Political Action Committee for Education:* This PAC prioritizes issues of the Indiana State Teachers Association including "creating a more equitable school funding formula" (Beck, 2022, para. 1). As of the final quarter of 2022, this PAC spent more than eight hundred thousand dollars in expenditures.
- *Liberty Defense PAC:* This PAC endorses candidates for school board and promotes "a 'no-compromise view on the issues of the sanctity of life, the 2nd amendment and religious freedom'" (Beck, 2022, para. 1). Through the first three quarters of 2022, this PAC spent more than ninety-six thousand dollars in expenditures.
- *Parents for Accountable Schools PAC:* Organized in one school district, this PAC "believes that parents are the ones who should be teaching social emotions (sic) skills and that schools should just focus on core subjects" (Beck, 2022, para. 1).
- *Support CCS:* This PAC prioritizes the purpose and practices of traditional public education in a school district. The website for this PAC indicates "we believe that public education is the foundation of a healthy democracy: accessible to all" (Support CCS, 2023).

Funding provided by PACs to candidates in local school board elections is a significant transformation of this small piece of democracy. Adult-centric partisanship competes on the funding playing field against student-centric school governance.

Local PACs dedicated to school board elections have "cousins" in the form of national PACs devoted, seemingly, to the adage that *all politics are local*. The 1776 Project PAC in the early 2020s, for instance, supported the successful campaigns of school board candidates who, subsequently, went "on to fire superintendents and enact sweeping 'bills of rights' for parents" (Binkley and Carr Smyth, 2022, para. 4).

Another national group with aspirations to influence local school board elections is the American Principles Project. Aiming its efforts at the election of candidates for local school boards, the American Principles Project's "fundraising average surged from under $50,000 the year before the pandemic to about $2 million now" (Binkley and Carr Smyth, 2022, para. 9).

Funding is weaponized to wrest governance of traditional public education from the hands of non-partisans.

This money supports consumer relations that offer views critical of those who support the curricular and instructional status quo in a school district. The website of a partisan Texas PAC put things this way: "We believe that the District's curriculum framework should be void of political partisanship and in keeping with conservative values" (Richman and Smith, 2022, para. 6).

Rarely do partisans acknowledge that "conservative values" are one and the same with political partisanship. When partisans control the governance of local education and are authorized to do so by state officials or legislation, the preferences and priorities of closely held beliefs and the individual proclivities of board members who espouse these beliefs eradicate the non-partisan ethos of traditional public education and a new balance is established for governance of teaching and learning in US schooling (Atterbury, 2022).

JUST HOW MUCH DOES ALL THIS COST?

There's a price tag attached to each major perspective about US education. Some of the costs associated with US education, like those discussed in relation to school board elections, are measured in dollars. Traditional public schools are funded by state and/or local taxes (Swensson, Lehman, and Ellis, 2021). Taxes, also, may pay directly or indirectly for partisan education.

Partisans contend that the cost of traditional public education is exorbitant and pays for extravagant, inefficient, and politically motivated teaching and learning. Partisan education is offered as a more efficient, less costly, brand of schooling.

Partisan education, in many cases, is funded by state taxes or tax avoidance mechanisms; partisan schools or families can be eligible to receive voucher or tax scholarship payments even when those families already can afford to pay private school tuition (Hinnefeld, 2023b; Swensson, Lehman, and Ellis, 2021).

Other costs associated with each major perspective are not paid by taxes but are no less contentious. For instance, partisans are adamantly opposed to the cost paid when citizens are forced to comply with government edicts including compulsory school attendance. "Liberty" is lost under these conditions.

Taking "Liberty" away from partisans is a cost of such magnitude that partisans unleash anarchic dissent to weaponize partisanship and eliminate the price paid when the capabilities for navigating precarious-balance are embedded in teaching and learning. For partisans, this means that citizenship education is one of the unnecessary costs of knowing along with others.

From the point of view of advocates for public education, however, these costs are justified. Reciprocity is invoked, for example, when individual rights are protected by government. The cost of citizenship that prompts government that works is acceptable because individual rights are part of an ethos dedicated to knowing along with others which nurtures shared concerns.

The price paid by students when partisanship controls teaching and learning is paid over time. When teaching and learning are restricted, students have limited, if any, engagement with the universe of discourse, *how to think*, and the common good. This price evaporates open futures for students.

The cost of partisan education goes beyond the damage done when mechanisms rob public schools of state funding. When open futures and the equity embedded in constitutional democracy are denied to students, children and young people pay when "the lack of equal and fair access to education, [means that] liberty becomes meaningless and democracy an empty concept capable of immediate devolution into aristocracy or plutocracy" (Imoukhuede, 2019, p. 447).

For society, partisan education exacts a substantial cost when the rule of law, the promises incorporated in founding documents from US history, and movement of the arc of the moral universe toward justice are taken off the market.

Simply put, partisanship will not pay for learning necessary to acquire the intellectual autonomy required to navigate precarious-balance. Partisans, further, will bear the cost of social reality as static-balance achieved when the goals of partisanship split winners from losers. Under the influence of closely held beliefs a divided social structure is not a cost but remuneration that pays partisans what they are worth.

To increase their "take," partisans promote cost avoidance, educational gerrymandering, and the defunding power of mechanisms to maximize the value from "Liberty." For partisans, costs and the personal economic decisions that avoid them are everywhere:

- Cost = Universal acceptance of citizens.
  - *Avoidance* = Universal singularity.
- Cost = Ideology/faith-neutrality.
  - *Avoidance* = Ideology/faith-centric.
- Cost = Precarious-balance.
  - *Avoidance* = Unlimited rights; static-balance.

Discarding equity, maximizing singularity, restricting the rights of "others"—all reflect the cost of partisanship throughout American history. The United States has long engaged in partisan "price wars" over religion, race, ethnicity, socioeconomic status, and political affiliation. In most instances, these battles originated when one sort of partisanship or another went in search of privilege (Suitts, 2016; Suitts, 2019).

At times during America's history, these impositions have been ballyhooed as "separate but equal." The imposition of partisanship and one comprehensive doctrine (Neufeld and Davis, 2010) in lieu of all others is the deliberate abrogation of civic respect. Partisanship wants no part of the public sector that values all comprehensive doctrines and that prioritizes reciprocity and concerns for others.

Partisans retreat from any cost associated with "others." Partisanship is unwilling to make payments for relational respect and knowing along with others. Identifying less cost as the right to social, economic, and/or political singularity, partisans turn away from the price they see in pluralism, diversity, and inclusion. Cost avoidance, in this case, is disdain for the pluralism of twenty-first-century America that is embraced in traditional public education.

Not only do partisans refuse to pay the ideological costs of reciprocity and the common good but they adamantly refuse the right of "others" to make their own choices when they want nothing to do with the dictates of partisanship. Under these circumstances, intellectual autonomy and the common good are eschewed in favor of partisans' "appeal to reasons that depend on the truth or correctness of their particular comprehensive doctrines" (Neufeld and Davis, 2010, p. 98).

Partisanship is a fine levied on the right of "others" who seek the best interests of their children in traditional public schools. Partisans augment this fee with the surcharge of anarchic dissent assessed when "others" pursue their own interests. Unwilling to pay the cost of knowing along with others and avoiding the cost of participatory citizenship along with others, partisans levy their imperatives on others.

The existence of traditional public education is, from a partisan's point of view, an unnecessary cost, an affront to closely held beliefs, and a denial of unlimited self-assigned rights. Partisanship has no interest in funding the pricey extravagances of traditional public education that establish connections and validate the rights of non-partisans.

A more complete assessment of the price of schooling in America leads to discussion of the role of religion, state legislatures, courts, and the federal government. All these elements of the public sector are involved when the major perspectives struggle to control who pays what, and why, for teaching and learning.

PART IV

Religion, Courts, the Feds, and Public Schools

Chapter 11

Evolution—The Faithful Sound the Alarm

Faith, from a partisanship perspective, is integral to every aspect of life. The faith-neutral ethos of traditional public education, as a result, is a price that partisans are unwilling to pay.

Illustrative of the degree to which partisans cannot abide this cost is the enmity directed toward the scientific principle of evolution. Evolution is not merely the topic that ignited a firestorm more than a century ago during the Scopes Monkey Trail. Evolution is an alarm bell in the night rousing twenty-first-century partisans to action.

The teaching of evolution, at the center of the Scopes Monkey Trail, became a *cause celebre* in 1925. A young public educator in Tennessee was taken to court for teaching evolution in contravention of a state statute that "prohibited instruction of 'any theory that denies the story of the divine creation of man as taught in the Bible'" (Salzman, 2022, p. 1072).

Deep-seated and faith-based then, deep-seated and faith-based in the twenty-first century, antipathy toward teaching and learning about evolution represents an integral piece of the revolt of the likeminded.

FAITHFUL PARTISANSHIP, EVOLUTION, AND LEARNING

Although the Scopes Monkey Trial is generally consigned to a brief mention in most history textbooks, evolution remains, for partisans, an enduring, and aggravating, symbol of faith-less teaching and learning in public schools: "A large portion of the North American public remains resistant, often resolutely so, to the notion of an evolutionary natural history, suggesting that they think scientists, teachers, and textbooks are simply wrong" (Wiles, 2010, para. 1).

Polls conducted in the first decade of the twenty-first century reveal that "over a span of 20 years, the percentage of adults in the U.S. who accept evolution declined from 45% to 40%" (Miller, Scott, and Okamoto, 2006, quoted in Wiles, 2010, para. 2).

Partisans turn to closely held beliefs where they find a self-evident article of faith to replace evolution. Advanced as if it's a scientific theory, "the religious doctrine of Intelligent Design Creationism" (Wiles, 2010, para. 5) is weaponized to end teaching and learning in public school classrooms about both evolution and the scientific method.

In the twenty-first century, rejection of and hostility toward science, and the academic base from which it generates knowledge, is integral to enduring skepticism about evolution. Not only is evolution considered to be the antithesis of intelligent design creationism, but instruction about evolution rubs salt in the wounds suffered by partisans when developments in society and in the court system push religion out of public schools.

For those opposed to intellectual autonomy, the tenets of comprehensive doctrine are far more valid than academic consensus about evolution.

What Science Says

Evolution, part of the instructional and scientific reality in public education, earns extensive validation from the scientific community. "The statement that organisms have descended with modifications from common ancestors—the historical reality of evolution—is not a theory. It is a fact, as fully as the fact of the earth's revolution about the sun" (Wiles, 2010, para. 5).

Despite such scholarly confirmation that evolution "is the scientific principle that the diversity of life on Earth has arisen via descent with modification from a common ancestry" (Wiles, 2010, para. 1), biological evolution continues to be doubted, maligned, and rejected by partisans.

ALARMING COURT DECISIONS

The push by partisans to incorporate faith within traditional public education—symbolized by enduring resistance to teaching about evolution—is not a twenty-first-century development. The history of faith and the history of traditional public education intertwine.

At one point in history, many US public schools held daily prayers aligned with the Christian faith. Public school calendars were built around Christian holidays. These practices reflected the comprehensive domain most closely aligned with partisanship which, then and now, is Protestant Christianity (Bindewald, 2015).

Whose Faith for Public Education?

When this comprehensive domain was an integral part of public education, students whose closely held beliefs were different had no recourse for expressing their faith and lacked the ability to opt out of this faith monopoly. As a matter of practice in public schools, the right of non-partisan students to freedom of religion was, at best, ignored, and, at worst, denied.

In response to several historic decisions by the US Supreme Court starting in the middle of the twentieth century, however, the presence of Protestant Christianity in traditional public schools faded:

- *Everson v. Board of Education* (1947): This decision "led to a wave of cases that severely restricted the power of the states and school districts to establish religion through educational policy" (Bates, 1993, pp. 45–46, quoted in Bindewald, 2015, p. 99).
- *McCollum v. Board of Education* (1948): The court ruled that a release-time program (students were released from class to meet on campus for devotional lessons) constituted a violation of the First Amendment. In the wake of *McCollum*, "released time participation nationwide saw a considerable decline" (Bindewald, 2015, p. 103).
- *Engel v. Vitale* (1962): This ruling found official school prayer to be a violation of the Establishment Clause and, therefore, unconstitutional.
- *Abington School District v. Schempp* (1963): The Court "forbade school-sponsored and devotional Bible reading" (Bindewald, 2015, p. 99). This ruling confirmed the observation that "separation of church and state means that the state is neutral towards religion. Setting aside school time for official prayer sessions is far from religious neutrality" (Farmer, 2001, para. 3).

  After this ruling, daily school-sponsored Christian prayer was no longer permitted. The court's decision encouraged a reconsideration of school calendars; observances of Christian holidays at school were relabeled as seasonal celebrations. As Farmer observes, *Schempp* "did *not* take prayer out of the school, it merely took government out of the business of prescribing religious exercises for students" (2001, para. 6).

The consequential impact of these decisions on the exercise of closely held beliefs in public schools led partisans to demand a return to the historic relationship between public education and faith.

Partisans called for a return to the days when "official prayers, daily readings from the King James Bible, and the use of materials that promoted a Protestant Christian worldview had become predominant features of common school culture throughout much of the United States" (Nord, 1995, quoted in Bindewald, 2015, p. 96).

Mourning the loss of a steadfast relationship between public education and faith, partisans fought back. "As American public schools gradually shifted away from a Protestant ethos toward a more secular approach to education, fundamentalists had to reconsider their strategic efforts to shape school policy and curriculum" (Bindewald, 2015, p. 103).

Expressing their intentions in slogans like "Put God Back in the Classroom," partisans staked their claim for reinstatement of a privileged faith in the practices of traditional public education.

Those who railed against court rulings that upheld the separation of church and state vowed to reassert the relationship between public schools and comprehensive doctrine as a right. "The culturally orthodox, whose stance is shaped by the assumption of a universal, external moral authority, gravitate toward a concern for bringing God back into the classroom (e.g., through school prayer)" (Sikkink, 1999, p. 59).

Dismayed by changes in US society and transfixed by the authority of the comprehensive domain in their own lives, partisans expressed outrage over the collapse of the relationship between faith and public education. Partisan leaders rallied the faithful to perceive this "'unbearable' situation as a call to action for the faithful to take the reins of the public schools" (Bindewald, 2015, p. 106).

Faithful partisans dedicated themselves to restoring their chosen comprehensive doctrine in public education. As Sikkink illustrates,

> evangelical thought and practice emphasizes the importance of religious presence in public institutions (Glenn 1987; Regnerus & Smith 1998; Sikkink 1998). The Evangelical sense of a custodial relationship of religion in relation to public life (Wacker, 1984) no doubt creates a greater sense of obligation to public schools, despite a high degree of alienation from them. (1999, p. 58)

Dominionism is another expression of faith committed to the presence of closely held beliefs within the practices of public education. This imperative for reasserting faith as part of learning in public schools is "sometimes referred to as the Seven Mountains Mandate, [which] is the belief that Christians are called on to dominate the seven key 'mountains' of American life, including business, media, government and education" (Hixenbaugh, 2022, para. 22).

To fulfill a faith-based obligation to public education, to dominate this "mountain" of life in America, partisans mobilized.

Putting Faith in the Courts

Judicial rulings that curtail the relationship between faith and public education are a source of partisan-based fury and despair. In response, some true believers channel their angst into support for free market mechanisms or private religious schools. For other partisans, dismay, anger, and righteous indignation inspire efforts to restore Protestant Christianity as an integral part of traditional public schooling.

Initially dismayed, nevertheless undaunted, faith-centered partisans paid attention to the power of the court system. Over time, comprehensive domains of partisanship emerged in rulings that seemed to favor a return of faith to public education:

- *Moss v. Spartanburg County School District Number 7* (2012): This federal court case found that "'the school district's release time policy was a passive measure aimed at satisfying the constitutionally permissible purpose of accommodating students' religious beliefs'" (Legal Clips, 2011, quoted in Bindewald, 2015, p. 104). This ruling established the constitutionality of release time programs held off school sites during regular school hours and deemed permissible the district's granting academic credit to participating students.
- *Kennedy v. Bremerton School District* (2022): The US Supreme Court found against a Seattle area public school district that fired an assistant football coach for kneeling to pray after games. The Court ruled that the coach's praying was a private act and that his termination violated the coach's free exercise and free expression rights. Shortly after this ruling, "families, teachers and activists are preparing to push religious worship into public schools nationwide—working to blur the line dividing prayer and pedagogy, and promising emotional, spiritual and educational benefits for students" (Natanson, 2022, para. 3).

Partisans encouraged by developments like these court cases do not prioritize government that works and, instead, attempt to prioritize religion that works for the restoration of partisanship in traditional public education and the outside world.

Chapter 12

Schools and Rights—Burdens, Exposure, and Compulsory Conduct

The meaning of the relationship between public education and faith develops when adherents of various religious faiths navigate the intersection of faith and education. Three generalizations summarize how faiths navigate this intersection.

- First, some religions operate private faith-based schools where religious instruction and learning in subject-area disciplines coexist. For instance, there are schools operated under the aegis of faith (i.e., the Catholic Church, the Lutheran Church) that have a significant presence throughout the United States. These schools engage students in learning both tenets of faith and subject area disciplines.
- Next, some religions offer private faith-based schools where religious instruction is prioritized and there is limited or no learning in the subject-area disciplines. Amish schools fit within this generalization. Operated by Amish communities, these schools focus on faith-based education that incorporates subject area disciplines most relevant to the Amish way of life (McConnell and Hurst, 2006). Schools operated for Hasidic Jewish students also represent this generalization. These schools, known as *yeshivas*, are operated by ultra-orthodox Jewish organizations. *Yeshiva* students engage fully with learning the Torah and experience only rudimentary learning in subject area disciplines (Shapiro and Rosenthal, 2022).
- Partisan education is a third generalization. Partisan education (featured in mechanisms like charter schools, virtual schools, and vouchers) incorporates the closely held principles and tenets of faith within partisanship. Partisans envision this brand of teaching and learning as the future

centerpiece of traditional public education. This final generalization is unique because partisanship is predicated on the goal of maintaining existing partisan schools while infiltrating closely held beliefs into traditional public schools (aka, government schools). Partisans navigate this intersection so that subject area disciplines reflect correspondence with tenets of Protestant Christianity, many of which are articulated in evangelism, foundationalism, and/or dominionism.

A TWO-PRONG TEST

Two questions can be posed to consider whether a practice of public education constitutes a burden on the free exercise or the free expression of religion. These questions constitute a filter through which court cases, and this discussion, can assess the extent to which a public school practice constitutes a burden on First Amendment freedoms:

1. "The threshold question asks whether or not the contested practice constitutes a real burden on the free exercise of religion" (Reich, 2002, p. 448).
2. "The balancing question asks, assuming a burden exists, whether or not compelling state interests exist that would outweigh the burden on free exercise" (Reich, 2002, p. 448).

This two-prong test came into play during *Wisconsin v. Yoder* (1972). The plaintiff alleged that compulsory attendance laws constituted a burden on the free expression of religion. Conversely, the state contended that compulsory attendance laws serve a compelling interest of the state and are not a burden.

Applying the threshold question involved determining whether compulsory attendance constituted a real burden on the free expression of religion by the Amish. An affirmative answer to this first question brought the balancing question into consideration.

The negative answer reached by the US Supreme Court to the balancing question (indicating that there was *no* compelling state interest that outweighed the burden on free exercise) led to the finding that, for the Amish, the contested practice (compulsory attendance) was an unconstitutional burden.

This ruling ended compulsory public school attendance by Amish students after grade eight. The ruling acknowledged that there is a compelling interest of government in compulsory attendance laws. But the application of the two-prong test confirmed that the compelled conduct constituted a real burden on the free exercise of the Amish religion.

This case does not represent, however, the only possible outcome when the two-prong test is invoked. A different court case (*Mozert v. Hawkins*) reveals that the two-prong test is responsive to each case. In *Mozert v. Hawkins*, plaintiffs challenged the constitutionality of a reading assignment required in a public school alleging that the assignment constituted a real burden on their free exercise of religion.

The court ruled, however, that the reading material required by the school district constituted *exposure* and not *compulsory conduct* (Reich, 2002). The compelling state interest (i.e., exposure to different reading levels and different topics for reading assignments) did not constitute a burden on free expression of religion. The fundamental distinction made by the court between exposure and compulsory conduct establishes benchmarks for consideration of issues relevant to this discussion.

The two-prong test presents a stiff challenge to partisans whose claims about closely held beliefs appear to indicate that partisanship is due the same status as any religion. By the same token, because they have religious underpinnings, partisan claims against public school practices deserve the same standing before the court as the Amish received.

The difficulty with such a claim is not merely the contention that partisanship deserves protection under the First Amendment like any other religion. On its face, asserting that partisanship is a religion strains credulity. Reflecting the finding from *Mozert v. Hawkins* sheds light on the specious nature of claims made by partisans that the compelling interests of government (e.g., exposure to the universe of discourse in public school curriculums/instruction) are a burden on the exclusive rights of partisanship.

Age-appropriate exposure (determined by professional educators who choose topics and instructional materials) to this immense array of topics, ideas, and issues is faith- and ideology-neutral. Exposure to the universe of discourse in a neutral learning environment is not an expectation, nor is it coercion, that compels student conduct.

Not only is exposure, without compelling conduct, essential to *how to think*, but *how to think* cannot be a burden on the non-religion known as partisanship.

Mozert stands as confirmation that the state has a compelling interest in the exposure of all students to the purpose of traditional public education. The compelling interest of the state in exposing students to this purpose does not burden the collectivist uniformity to which partisans, alone, assign a faith-equivalent status.

Despite the claims made by partisans, the state has no compelling interest in what-to-think. Rather, the compelling interest of the state is in exposure to intellectual autonomy in the universe of discourse that permits individual choice to permit both an open future for every student and the right to participatory citizenship.

One of the enduring paradoxes that accompanies partisanship emerges when proponents of partisan education turn ideological- and faith-neutrality into a burden and, simultaneously, impose compulsory conduct and closely held beliefs on non-partisan students as reform of public education.

Partisans project onto public schooling their allegation that public education denies free expression. The imposition of partisan education compels students whose religious beliefs and/or ideological principles do not conform to the expectations of partisanship to accept a true burden on free expression and free exercise.

Partisan education is not mere exposure. Rather, partisan education compels conduct and, as if in answer to the threshold question of the two-prong test, partisan education brazenly burdens non-partisans. The adult-centric ethos of partisan education constitutes what amounts to a compelling interest of *non*-government.

Partisanship, per se, has no authority to compel any educational practice. Ostensibly, partisan education cannot "pass" the two-prong test.

But legislators in some states in the twenty-first century exercise their authority to impose partisanship (i.e., ban books and restrict classroom topics) without paying heed to the implications that can be derived from the two-prong test. If non-partisans were to provide an answer to the threshold question for partisan legislators, this response would reveal that the imposition of faith-centered partisanship *is* a burden on free expression.

At the foundation of partisanship is one comprehensive doctrine. The intention of partisans is to restore this doctrine to the practices of traditional public education without regard for the diversity and pluralism that public schools welcome and nurture. Compelling non-partisans to forsake expression of their faiths under the mandates imposed by partisan education reveals the real intention of partisanship to create a real burden on "others" that is justified because it is what is right and what is true.

Partisans burden non-partisans when closely held beliefs pretend to represent the best interests of children but blithely ignore that "in vindicating their own Free Exercise rights, the parents usurp those of their children by compelling them to accept an education that precludes exposure to diverse ideas and ways of life" (Reich, 2002, p. 455).

Paying no attention to the threshold question in the two-prong test, partisans also ignore the answer to the balancing question. Partisans contend, in response to the balancing question, that there is no compelling interest of the state that outweighs the exclusive rights of partisanship when they are imposed on "others." Partisans may argue, as did a King of France, *L'etat, C'est moi!* ("I am the state"), but a claim to this right of kings is a fundamental violation of the rights of all citizens in our constitutional democracy.

From a partisan's point of view, this "royal" expression of partisanship aligns perfectly with universal singularity and unlimited individual rights for partisans. Thus, partisan legislators are acting not on behalf of the state or government but on behalf of the loosely coupled end-state sought by partisans on their own behalf. After all, less government and/or no government is a primary goal for partisans.

For partisans, lessons found in judicial decisions that illuminate the relationship between education and First Amendment guarantees are irrelevant. But these lessons illustrate the capricious, self-serving focus of partisan education and the statutes promulgated on its behalf:

- *Exposure to ideas/topics* in public education (*Mozert*) is not the same as *the burden imposed* on free exercise by compulsory conduct (*Yoder*).
- Traditional public education engages students with exposure to ideas à la *Mozert*; partisan education imposes closely held beliefs as burdens on teaching à la *Yoder*.
- Neither religion nor government, partisanship is the assumption that reform of traditional public education (e.g., the return of comprehensive doctrine; the alignment of curriculum and instruction with partisanship-approved topics) *un*-burdens students and *exposes* the present-day coercion in public schools where students are compelled to experience intellectual autonomy in contravention of the compelling interest of partisanship in static-balance.
- The two-prong test is a bankrupt assessment of partisan education because the comprehensive doctrine at the base of partisanship constitutes a compelling interest that cannot burden any citizen because the universal singularity pursued in partisan education is what is right and what is true.

WHEN PUBLIC EDUCATION MEETS THE US CONSTITUTION

Partisans insist that their right to cultural self-determination takes precedence over compelling governmental interest in the purpose of traditional public education and supersedes the rights of "others" whose beliefs do not correspond with those of partisans.

Claiming an absolute right to cultural self-determination, partisanship is given a status equivalent to an enumerated right so that partisans give themselves, as a result, status as a protected class. This status is sufficient to override diversity, contemporary social reality, and non-partisan interpretations of the rule of law.

The certainties claimed on behalf of partisanship and the presumption that partisans are the equivalent of a protected class border on delusion.

In part, these delusions may be rooted in the fact that there is no right to education contained in the US Constitution. No portion of this document mentions public education, its purpose, or its value to democracy (Hartman, 2005). Education is one of many unenumerated rights.

Even though unenumerated rights are granted to the states, some are recognized among the nation's fundamental rights. For example, the right to privacy is "so rooted in the nation's history and traditions that the Supreme Court recognizes them as fundamental" (Imoukhuede, 2019, p. 445).

Education, however, has never been recognized in this way. In fact, the opposite is true. The US Supreme Court ruled that there is no federal guarantee to a right to public education (*San Antonio Independent School District v. Rodriguez*, 1973).

These details may undergird the partisan reasoning that action by a state legislature to deal with an unenumerated right (education) can be justified if such action supports enumerated rights (e.g., free expression/exercise of religion) and if such action aligns with fundamental rights (privacy).

On the other hand, the value of public education in a democracy has been recognized by the US Supreme Court. In *Brown v. Board of Education* (1956), the Court wrote that education "is the very foundation of good citizenship. Today it is a principal instrument in awakening the child to cultural values, in preparing him for later professional training, and in helping him to adjust normally to his environment" (Hartman, 2005, p. 100).

Although this statement identifies the impact of traditional public education, judicial consideration of contested educational issues is ongoing, and unasked questions exist. It is possible, for example, that future rulings that may influence whether education is a right and, therefore, subject to an obligation to act by the US government.

In terms of the struggle between the two major perspectives about US education, the involvement of the courts is both an important element of decision-making in a constitutional democracy and involvement of the courts can be a complicating factor.

After all, judicial interpretations are partly responsible for both the glacial pace of America's historic journey to bring its foundational principles into practice and for the often-dramatic pedal-to-the-metal acceleration that brings these principles to the proverbial finish line.

For example, if a case arose that did contest whether traditional public education is a fundamental right, it might be possible to ask: If "recognizing a fundamental right to public education would arguably require the government to fulfill a duty while protecting a fundamental liberty—the freedom from ignorance" (Imoukhuede, 2019, p. 445)?

THE US SUPREME COURT AND US EDUCATION

Although it is beyond the scope of this discussion to deal with the full range of Supreme Court decisions that influence US education, some notable cases hint at the relevance of judicial findings to the contemporary imbroglio over teaching and learning in America.

Frequently at issue when a verdict influences US education are the rights guaranteed by various amendments to the US Constitution.

The First Amendment

Public education engages all students with the cognitive, creative, practical, and emotional intelligences required for participatory citizenship. The rights of individuals to receive what public schools teach, and the compelling interest of the state to determine this learning, are often addressed in rulings about freedom of speech.

To understand freedom of speech as it is articulated in the First Amendment of the US Constitution is no simple matter. Virtually since its inception, the US Supreme Court has wrestled with interpretations of freedom of speech. Some of these interpretations directly affect the nature of teaching and learning.

Hazelwood School District v. Kuhlmeier

Public educators and those who support traditional public education as a pillar of constitutional democracy turn to the First Amendment to verify the central role of government in public schooling. The First Amendment "does not afford an individual's right to dictate the conduct of the Government's internal procedures" (Bowie, 2019, p. 50). This puts public education authorities, as agents of the state, in position to make decisions about "legitimate pedagogical concerns" (Salzman, 2022, p. 1077).

To this end, in *Hazelwood School District v. Kuhlmeier* (1988), the Supreme Court "answered a narrow question: Under what circumstances may school authorities regulate student speech in curricular contexts such as school newspapers, exams, and essays?" (Salzman 2022, p. 1078). In answer to this question, the court determined that public schools are permitted "to restrict students' expression in curricular settings . . . [when] ensuring that students learn the intended lessons" (Salzman, 2022, p. 1077).

But this ruling, and other opinions rendered by the courts, view the extremely broad intersection between freedom of speech and public schools with the judicial equivalent of a peep hole. Overall, "the Supreme Court has not directly addressed what limitations—if any—are imposed on local curricular authorities by the First Amendment" (Salzman, 2022, pp. 1076–77).

Moreover, *Hazelwood* does not establish "outer limits on state speech in the closed school environment" (Salzman, 2022, p. 1078). "Lower courts have extended this logic to the educational sphere, explaining that schools—as state entities—are entitled to regulate the content of what is expressed when they speak" (Salzman, 2022, p. 1076).

This point of view validates the authority of boards of education and public educators as agents of the state to act as the rightful source of curricular content. The Court indicated that "school boards execute 'important, delicate, and highly discretionary functions,' which come with substantial community benefits" (Salzman, 2022, p. 1075). This small piece of democracy is given license to attend to and meet the needs of the community it serves.

Board of Education v. Pico

Partisan efforts to take control of public school governance reflect the assumption that school boards have complete control of teaching and learning. Partisans might, after reflecting on the ruling in *Hazelwood*, believe that taking control of a school board opens the door to any and all aspects of partisan education. It turns out, however, that the authority of the state, in the form of locally elected school boards, is not all-encompassing.

In *Board of Education v. Pico* (1979), the court limited the authority of a school board to remove books from a school library. A school board, the Court held, "could not remove books from a school library simply because it considered the books 'anti-American, anti-Christian, anti-Semitic, and just plain filthy'" (Bindewald, 2015; Salzman, 2022, p. 1080).

This ruling invoked the First Amendment in the sense that students have a right to receive ideas and information. "The *Pico* Court held that school authorities may not constitutionally censor selected books from public school libraries 'in a narrowly partisan or political manner'" (Salzman, 2022, p. 1079).

Students, thus, have a right under the First Amendment to receive communicated speech represented by books in a school library. This premise guides the response to contemporary state statutes that "are so broadly worded as to chill free speech" (Natanson, 2023b, para. 19). Lawsuits that pursue this reasoning argue that state statutes are riddled with vague language that ensures an "alarming degree of subjectivity with regard to whether something . . . is really patently offensive" (Natanson, 2023b, para. 20).

Substantial constitutional barriers stand in the way of partisan efforts to limit the message of content chosen by school authorities for teaching and learning. Additional court rulings prevent statutory efforts to chill the free speech provided in books. It turns out that public schools have the right to determine the speech represented in curriculum and instruction while public school governance may not limit the right of students to receive communicated speech.

The Third Amendment

Advocates of the supremacy of parental rights turn to both common law and interpretations of the Bill of Rights to justify the legal standing of parents/caregivers to direct what happens in public education (Klicka and Phillips, 1997).

In theory, this power could be used by partisans and non-partisans alike to validate the right of parents/caregivers to control the positive recognition of, and protection for, children and young people whose "I identify as . . ." statements make them targets of discrimination, hate, and denial of rights (Swensson, Ellis, and Shaffer, 2019b).

In theory, parental rights could signal a unity of purpose among family adults to ensure equitable treatment of all students in all situations in the nation's public schools. In theory, parents and caregivers aligned with partisanship ideals could emphasize their rights to direct their children in organizations or entities that *already exist* as sectarian or private schools where closely held beliefs and partisanship, properly, are the order of the day.

But in practice, as this discussion reveals, partisans have no interest in concerns for others, reciprocity, or the common good. As critics of Moms for Liberty and other likeminded groups indicate, the "'parental rights' movement [serves] as code for intolerance to ideas like LGBTQ student rights and a full teaching of the nation's racist past" (Solochek, 2022, para. 8).

Proponents of partisan education justify the right to inject full parental rights into any school by referring to the Third Amendment and its prohibition against quartering troops in private homes. Partisans interpret this amendment as attending to parental rights because "one finds the simple principle [in the Third Amendment] that agents of the state should hold the sanctity of the home inviolable" (Klicka and Phillips, 1997, p. 82).

Agents of the state, given this logic, are at the beck and call of parental assumptions, beliefs, fantasies, demands, and theories. Partisans contend that the inviolable sanctity of the home extends to the classroom where school personnel, as agents of the state, are precluded from decisions and actions that do not comply with absolute parental rights.

It comes as no surprise, therefore, that partisans convince themselves that "parents' rights are inviolable, that is, that the government has absolutely no right to dictate *anything* to parents and that the school, therefore, has no right to impose any curriculum, content, or requirement that parents object to" (emphasis original) (Burron, 1996, p. 81).

Taken literally, this perspective invites and justifies anarchic dissent as a response to any failure of public schools to live up to the partisan interpretation of the Third Amendment. Parents/caregivers and the proponents of partisan education give themselves absolute veto power over existing school practices. Partisans assume this power is a right to dictate to and interfere with any aspect or decision made in the public sector with which they disagree.

The inviolability of parental rights derived from the sanctity of the home is the launching pad for the partisan transformation of teaching and learning in public schools. If this right is not acknowledged to the satisfaction of partisans, then any action is justified to install the inviolable home into public school classrooms.

The Fourteenth Amendment

Parental rights are held forth by partisans as a greater good than the common good based on precedents from history that influence the US Constitution (Sedler, 2006). But this greater good is upended when states enact "statutes making education compulsory and imposing the duty on parents to enroll their children in the public or private schools" (Sedler, 2006, p. 5).

Ignoring the fact that such statutes were enacted in accordance with obligations established by state constitutions, proponents of the absolute authority of parents contend that public schooling is one of the "things that no government, no matter how democratically elected, should be able to do to those it governed" (Sedler, 2006, p. 6). Such absolutist declarations ignore, of course, that state constitutions and government that works are constructs of the governed.

Partisanship invokes its closely held beliefs and interpretations of the US Constitution against government that *does things* to partisans (e.g., public education) that are impermissible, illegal violations of unlimited individual rights. True believers in the inviolability of parental rights find support for their battle against government that works in some US Supreme Court rulings.

For instance, partisans highlight that "the Fourteenth Amendment's due process clause has been used by the Supreme Court to create a constitutional right of parents to control the education of their children" (Sedler, 2006, p. 2).

Believing that government works against people and denies the rights that partisanship assigns to true believers, partisans disconnect from the rule of law. Casting themselves as subject to uncontrollable nefarious forces, partisans denounce majority rule in favor of their self-proclaimed right to supersede "others." Inviolability permits partisans to deny to "others" the rights claimed as the exclusive property of partisans. Partisanship is minority rule.

The absolutist and collectivist intentions of partisan education infuse the priorities of partisanship with inviolability. Tilting toward universal singularity and intending that government will not work, partisan education terminates the work in progress that is both the purpose of public education and the nature of constitutional democracy. Because government is worthless, partisanship operationalizes static-balance to ensure that no interest of government compels individuals to do anything.

Conversely, construction of the intersection between individual rights and public education as an exemplar of the compelling interests of government evolves from intellectual autonomy. This intersection facilitates the parental interests that are incorporated throughout traditional public education:

- Parents' right to control education are "subject to reasonable regulation by the state in order to advance the state's compelling interest in ensuring that the child receives a fully adequate education" (Sedler, 2006, p. 12).
- The work in progress nature of this balance hearkens to the Supreme Court ruling that "while a student may sometimes be 'forced to speak or write on a particular topic even though the student might prefer a different topic,' public schools 'may not demand that a student profess beliefs or views with which the student does not agree'" (Salzman, 2022, pp. 1083–84).
- Public education's purpose is to expose students to the universe of discourse and not to compel behavior that is antithetical to parental interests or comprehensive doctrine of the family. In an ideological- and faith-neutral learning environment, students are not compelled to profess what they don't believe. In partisan education, the opposite is true.

One example illustrates the impact when the equal protection clause of the Fourteenth Amendment comes into play. In this instance, suit was filed against a school district's decision to remove ten books that dealt with topics about the LGBTQ community and race.

The lawsuit filed against the district claimed a violation of the equal protection clause "because the books being singled out for possible removal are disproportionately books by non-white and/or LGBTQ authors, or which address topics related to race or LGBTQ identity" (Yurcaba, 2023, para. 4).

Plaintiffs in this case noted that discriminatory actions like these cannot be the basis for government action.

When government works and the purpose of traditional public education is an investment in capabilities that navigate precarious-balance, public education is society's "attempt to ensure that every student has an experience that elevates their opportunity, that validates their identity, that ensures engagement and curiosity" (Pendharkar, 2022, para. 2).

Future lawsuits and future rulings by the judiciary will continue to influence both major perspectives about US education. All future court action, regardless of outcome, will determine how instruction is delivered, how learning is measured, how education accommodates the belief systems and lifeviews of its citizens, and how government works in response to the outcomes created by students when they become voters.

Chapter 13

To Reform or Not to Reform?

To reform education in the name of partisanship or not to reform education in the name of partisanship? That is the question. Is orthodoxy for education the future or will the purpose of traditional public education continue to educate nine out of ten US students?

Reform, a partisan cudgel used to bash traditional public education, is the assumption of a right to reject practices and principles that do not evince closely held beliefs. The appeal of reform for partisans is found in its promise to bind teaching and learning to the collectivist perspective that is partisanship.

The collectivist perspective of partisanship is an *alliance with certainty*. In partisan-friendly terms, this alliance is expressed in a total disregard for what is right and what is true for "others." Mustered to alleviate fear and to impose orthodoxy, the alliance of certainty cements reform to purpose of partisan education.

Preying on fears of family adults while offering the salve of orthodoxy—the certainties in partisanship—reform is a cure for characteristics, fears, incidents, or concerns associated with traditional public school.

Once shoppers buy-in to partisan education, my-side bias upholds the charade that reform is a necessity. My-side bias recycles the value of commitment to boutique-ideology in terms familiar to and supportive of partisanship. Moreover, synergy of struggle transforms the fears of parents/caregivers into certainty via the collectivist feedback loop that validates partisan consciousness about what is right and what is true.

Tang (2018) succinctly reiterates the dilemma embedded in the imposition of partisanship on public schooling. When partisans enter an alliance with certainty, education becomes a box canyon from which non-partisans have no exit: If "parents should be viewed 'primarily as potential instruments of the child's welfare; [then] the chief issue is whether [parental] choice would be a blessing for [all] children'" (Tang, 2018, p. 354).

What is right, what is true, "Liberty," and transparency—all are brand names sold under the label of reform in the educational marketplace. Fearful that these brands are scarce commodities, proponents of partisanship rally the likeminded to secure the right to shop for orthodoxy.

Orthodoxy for education provides shoppers with common sense, what-to-think, parental rights, and "Liberty." Fear evaporates if it is possible to buy brand name certainties. The alliance of certainty fends off the intrusions of government and the social reality where "others" might thrive. Reform fulfills best interests riveted to what is right and what is true; the exclusionary ethos at the core of partisanship flourishes under these conditions.

THE DESTINATION IS REFORM. ARE WE THERE YET?

Within the exclusionary confines of partisan education, what is right and what is true are implemented to ensure learning is aligned with *being in the world but not of the world*.

Partisan education assures shoppers that teaching and learning do not conform with governmental edicts or faith-neutral teaching and learning. Orthodoxy for education is a guarantee that curriculum, instruction, and learning will not stray from the destination of static-balance. Being in the world necessitates reform to establish teaching and learning that is seamlessly aligned with the principles and tenets of partisanship.

I'M FREE TO BE ME AND YOU'RE FREE TO BE ME

In the twenty-first century, partisans clearly convey their "'general sense of unease with some of the cultural direction of contemporary public education'" (Richman and Smith, 2022, para. 13). Boutique-ideology, the repository of the truths in partisanship, is imposed on public schools to "help restore some common sense and American social, moral and academic values" (Herron and Beck, 2022, p. 12A).

Partisans understand their "Liberty" is their right to impose. The imposition of partisanship on learning is the right to eschew knowing along with others. Unsullied by contact with "others" and their unorthodox beliefs, partisans claim exclusive access to what is right and what is true without regard for, or understanding of, liberty due to others. "Liberty" is invoked as a partisan's right to partisanship and the obligation of "others" to comply with partisanship.

PARTISANS ARE *THE PUBLIC*

Walled off from "others" and detached from the outside world, partisans invent themselves as the rightful version of *the public* in America. Free to ignore, disdain, and reject "others," *the public* is reformed as an exclusive coterie of shoppers. "The customer role is more aligned with the ability to secure one's own individual liberty, rather than an interest in the wellbeing or equality of the community or the process of democratization" (Stitzlein, 2015, p. 68).

Holding closely held beliefs, *the public* posits the orthodoxy of marketplace singularity as sufficient for determining that the public sector, including public education, is worthless. "Liberty" gives partisans the right to disconnect from the public sector.

But the ubiquity of the public sector, and the extensive number of citizens who support traditional public education, stand in the way of partisans as *the public* and the intentions to replace contemporary social reality with the social consciousness of universal singularity. To eliminate the threat posed by worthless public things and to dislodge the contemporary social structure that is very much *in* and *of* the outside world, partisans invest in a social consciousness apart from contemporary social reality, the public sector, government that works, and concerns for others.

The social consciousness of partisanship evokes a paraphrase of Robert Frost (1942): *Good fences make good partisans*. Partisanship is an acute awareness of the threats in contemporary social reality that require fencing off the outside world and the intrusions of non-partisans.

Principles of ideology and tenets of faith are the materials used to construct this fence. Fence builders fashion anarchic dissent, public dissonance, free market theory, and boutique-ideology to isolate partisans from the malign influences of the outside world and from the disastrous uncertainties of precarious-balance.

Parents and caregivers who are already disposed to look at government schools with trepidation find value in fences that separate *the public* from traditional public education where neutrality and *how to think* on behalf of the common good lie in wait to infect the thinking and behavior of students from partisan families.

Warding off beliefs of "others" and any perspective inconsistent with education for orthodoxy, partisans build fences to safeguard the exercise of their "Liberty." These responses, perceptions, and fences are partisan things, the inviolabilities of reform.

Partisan Things Are Not Public Things

Traditional public education is *a public thing*. Public things are "those material objects and spaces that are a shared and intractable part of democratic life" (Knight Abowitz, 2018, p. 8).

Public education and all other public things are premised on reciprocity which is necessary and sufficient to facilitate "fair social cooperation amongst all citizens" (Neufeld and Davis, 2010, p. 107). The necessary parts of democratic life entail autonomy, collaboration, individual rights, compelling interests of government, equity, and fair social cooperation.

Every aspect of democratic life exists amid precarious-balance which, by its nature is intractable or hard to control. Government that works, constitutional democracy, the public sector, and traditional public education are hard to control.

The value of traditional public education as a public thing is expressed when the purpose of public schools engages all students with the capabilities for recognizing, then navigating, the precarious-balance the intractability of the tension between diversity and unity.

The worth of participatory citizenship depends upon citizens capable of monitoring and navigating precarious-balance in pursuit of government that works. Seeking, monitoring, and adjusting are required for government that works in response to the tension between diversity and unity. Like navigating precarious balance, this tension is hard to control but is an unavoidable characteristic of pluralism in constitutional democracy.

Diverse perspectives are engendered by *how to think* on behalf of the common good. As a shared and intractable part of democratic life, public education facilitates participatory citizenship through which all citizens may cooperate fairly. Of course, fair social cooperation is not a statement that universal agreement is achieved. Rather, fair social cooperation reflects the rule of law suffused with balance-as-equity to mediate intractability.

But, as these constructs and descriptors illustrate, partisan things are not public things. Partisan things are those material things and spaces that fence off, disconnect from, or dispose of the intractability in democratic life.

Partisan things are carved out of the social consciousness that demands absolute control exercised by the few who adhere to the collectivist consciousness of partisanship. Partisan things abandon fair social cooperation. Partisan things invest in certainty. Partisan things seek static-balance. Partisan things retreat from conscience with predictable results:

> In the absence of different perspectives and a wide range of information, the system cannot function. It will fail to expose errors of fact. It will fail to shed

the kind of light that comes only from diverse perspectives about public issues. (Salzman, 2022, p. 1087)

Because partisan things function in a closed system, barriers are a priority.

Partisan things do not recognize the value of a wide range of information; a system imbued with partisanship functions in the absence of diverse perspectives. Static-balance is a destination that ignores the tension between diversity and unity. The partisan fence line deters errors of fact because such errors are impossible from education and in social reality anchored by the self-evident.

The function of partisan things spells the demise of public things. The demise of public things ensures the dominance of universal singularity. Universal singularity ensures the unraveling of government that works. Partisan things function to separate learning from the common good and disconnect the common good from the rights of "others."

WHEN REFORM IS NOT PARTISAN

Earlier in this discussion, two examples of partisan education conducted in the name of faith—Amish schools and Hasidic *yeshivas*—shed light on partisan education that does not impose closely held beliefs on "others." These exemplars demonstrate that partisanship per se does not require educational reform that nullifies rights, ideologies, and faiths of non-partisans.

The Amish and Reform

State of Wisconsin v. Jonas Yoder et al. is the 1972 decision by the US Supreme Court that exempted "the Amish from compulsory schooling beyond eighth grade" (McConnell and Hurst, 2006, p. 236). In this ruling, the court concluded that "enforcement of the State's compulsory formal education after eighth grade would gravely endanger if not destroy the free exercise of respondents' religious beliefs" (McConnell and Hurst, 2006, p. 236).

The court's ruling took account of the *consistent practice* and *sustained faith* necessary to the continuity of community in Amish lives. So unique is the Amish way of life, and this uniqueness is so integrated with their religious beliefs, that mandating public school attendance for Amish children beyond the eighth grade was determined to be nothing less than denial of the free exercise of religion.

As an instance where the two-prong test worked in favor of the plaintiffs, the court's finding prioritized the free exercise of religion over the compelling interest of government.

In the Aftermath of Yoder

The validation of "cultural self-determination through control of education" is the way researchers describe the impact of *Wisconsin v. Yoder* (McConnell and Hurst, 2006, p. 236). *Yoder* "opened the door for the proliferation of private Amish schools, which in 2004 numbered 1,316 and catered to 35,863 students in more than 20 states" (Ohio Amish Directory, 2005, p. xvii, quoted in McConnell and Hurst, 2006, p. 236).

These schools offered curriculum and instruction that featured "the practical application of schoolwork and [placed emphasis] on the importance of physical labor" (McConnell and Hurst, 2006, p. 242). Amish schools offer teaching and learning—including study in traditional subjects—that is consistent with and necessary for sustaining the unique and historic interconnection between Amish faith and culture:

> This high degree of cultural cohesion and insularity is one factor behind the relative success they have had in resisting mainstream schooling compared to other ethnic-religious minorities, though their "economic self-sufficiency" and "residential independence" have also played key roles. (Dewalt and Troxell, 1989, p. 308, quoted in McConnell and Hurst, 2006, p. 249)

Amish schools are a resource dedicated to "the purpose of keeping their community intact and tightly integrated" (McConnell and Hurst, 2006, p. 249). In the aftermath of *Yoder*, the Amish took control of education to ensure cultural self-determination. Preserving and nurturing the exercise of their faith within their institutions and social structure, the Amish hold fast to their closely held beliefs without imposing on traditional public education, social reality, or government that works.

Hasidic Communities and Reform

Yeshivas are private schools, segregated by gender, operated by the Hasidic Jewish community in the New York City area. *Yeshivas* are another example of education conducted through the auspices of a religious faith.

These schools offer little or no instruction in traditional subject areas. *Yeshivas* eschew connections with learning associated with the outside world. Scores of these schools exist "to educate students in Jewish law, prayer, and tradition—and to wall them off from the secular world" (Shapiro and Rosenthal, 2022, para. 4).

It's important to note that for most in the Hasidic community, "their schools are succeeding—just not according to the standards set by the outside world. In a community that places religion at the center of daily life, secular education is often viewed as unnecessary, or even distracting" (Shapiro and Rosenthal, 2022, para. 23). Like Amish schools, education for Hasidic students is conducted in the interest of religious and cultural self-determination.

Students educated in *yeshivas* are not expected to have much of a life "in the world" and, certainly, no life "of the world." The outside world is irrelevant and so are its academic disciplines, topics, issues, and concerns. Like many other private schools operated on behalf of a religion, *yeshivas* do not force their purpose or practices onto traditional public schools.

In the Aftermath of Yeshiva Education

In the aftermath of a *yeshiva* education, "students grow up and can barely support their own families" (Shapiro and Rosenthal, 2022, para. 20). Paltry opportunities for learning traditional academic disciplines (after school hours, four days a week, for students aged eight through twelve) ensure that *yeshiva* students leave school "without learning to speak English fluently, let alone read or write at grade level" (Shapiro and Rosenthal, 2022, para. 6).

Yeshivas "turn out thousands of students each year who are unprepared to navigate the outside world, helping to push poverty rates in Hasidic neighborhoods to some of the highest in New York" (Shapiro and Rosenthal, 2022, para. 7).

THE COMPELLING INTERESTS OF PARTISANSHIP

Both Amish schools and *yeshivas* pursue teaching and learning on behalf of closely held beliefs. For the Amish, Hasidic Jews, and several other religions that operate faith-based schools, there is no interest in imposing faith on public education or any other element of the public sector. The tradition of separation of church and state serves the interests of both the faithful and those in society who are non-partisans.

But, as this discussion illustrates, the compelling interests of partisanship express different intentions and, in so doing, resemble the relentless pack ice that surrounded *Endurance*, the boat used by Ernest Shackleton to sail to Antarctica in 1914.

In the Weddell Sea, approaching Antarctica, the *Endurance* came to a halt, trapped by unforgiving pack ice. Unable to free *Endurance* from the ice, Shackelford and his entire crew floated away to safety on ice floes and in lifeboats. *Endurance*, crushed, sank.

Like the ice pack that immobilized, then destroyed, *Endurance*, the compelling interests of partisanship surround traditional public education. The compelling interests of partisanship push against the purpose of public schools and the social reality of which public education is part. The compelling interests of partisanship move relentlessly to crush public schools:

- Partisans gerrymander funding away from public schools and direct state dollars to partisan mechanisms: insufficient fiscal support for public education is a compelling interest of partisanship.
- After restricting intellectual autonomy, advocates of partisan education push against public schools and ask why students are so unprepared for employment. Advocates for partisan education float to safety on consumer relations that claim exemplary educational results that accrue for students when ideology guides teaching and learning.
- Imposing low-cost and less government, partisanship squeezes traditional public schools between these compelling interests to suppress the number and quality of individuals who become public educators.
- Unconvinced about the value of the time-honored phrase, *you get what you pay for*, proponents of the educational marketplace surround public education with "unequal access to educational resources; inadequate funding for schools; stagnant compensation for teachers; heavier workloads; declining prestige; and deteriorating faculty morale" (Edsall, 2022, para. 1).
- Partisan things deter college students from enrolling in teacher preparation programs and sink the number of graduates needed to offer all students quality teaching and learning in the future of public education.
- Partisanship further closes in around public education when licensure requirements for educators are eliminated or diminished, virtual learning is prioritized, and the content of classroom discourse in public schools is censored. These compelling interests dumb down learning.

Combined with inadequate compensation for public educators, dumbed down learning restricts the future for students of color and students in poverty. Crushed by dumbed down instruction and denied the capabilities required for intellectual autonomy, the futures of public school students are immobilized by the compelling interests of partisanship.

In addition, dumbed down preparation and inadequate compensation are compelling interests that combine to create a teacher shortage crisis in the twenty-first century. This ongoing dilemma mirrors similar crises that have plagued public education in the past. For example, in "Oklahoma and Arizona, those crises existed long before 2020, driven in part by low teacher pay, cuts to school spending, and less interest in the teaching profession" (Balingit, 2022, para. 3).

Partisanship traps teaching and learning in a destination where closely held beliefs are imposed on behalf of static-balance. Just as pack ice ended the voyage of *Endurance*, partisanship immobilizes the journey of public education and, just like the Shackleton expedition, partisanship crushes the purpose and practices of public schools between obdurate ideological ice floes that can be labeled as:

- *A world apart:* Partisans identify a significant mismatch between partisan education and the purpose of US public education. Ideologies and religions "desire to retain a certain 'ideal' world, while the school's emphasis is on the need to adapt to the 'real' world" (McConnell and Hurst, 2006, p. 250). Partisanship emphasizes the capacities for a social reality that is a world apart from the rights, beliefs, faiths, and identities cherished by non-partisans. Separation and the inviolability of universal singularity speak to the world apart enforced through partisanship.
- *Truncated freedom:* "Liberty," as it is defined through partisanship, tilts the all-citizens guarantees found in the First Amendment away from equity and toward exclusion. The faith-neutral stance of public schools is a commitment to the free exercise and free expression of religion as one guarantor for the pluralism of US society represented in the diversity of student enrollment in traditional public schools. Freedom of expression and freedom of exercise of religion are smashed, however, when partisanship commits to one faith. Partisan education represents the imposition of one faith in public education without regard for or protection of the religious beliefs of non-partisans. Freedom of expression and freedom of exercise for "others" sink.
- *Public sector nihilism:* From the perspective of partisans, the public sector is meaningless. Government, public education, and all other entities that comprise the public sector have no value. Traditional public education is valueless because it does not prioritize a collectivist consciousness. Partisans embrace boutique-ideology because it is liberated from knowing along with others which, in turn, renders participatory citizenship and constitutional democracy meaningless. Partisan education acquires meaning when students learn and act in accordance with survival of the fittest and economic one-upmanship. Rejecting traditional public schools as meaningless, partisans offer learning that establishes meaning-making in an ideal world unfettered by the common good but secured by absolutist compelling interests. Public sector nihilism is the certainty about what's meaningless that protects partisanship from unorthodox intrusions.
- *Self-aggrandizing citizenship:* The closely held beliefs that require separation from "others" for their full implementation are given carte blanche to partisan education to exclude. Because partisan schooling embraces

an *every man for himself* view of learning, and because this view is the stipulation that predesignated winners succeed, amorality in the educational marketplace and disdain for equity represent compelling interests of partisans in acquisitive citizenship. The extremes of partisanship fuel self-aggrandizing citizenship in lieu of participatory citizenship.

Compelling interests of partisanship dictate that government that works is meaningless. Government that works is an oxymoron from the perspective of partisans because a working government erodes the inviolability of orthodoxy, disassembles universal singularity, and tramples the unlimited rights due only to partisans.

Partisan education requires what amounts to *auto-evaporating government*. Once crushing traditional public education in the name of the compelling interests of partisanship is complete, the worthless nature of government comes to the fore and government that works disappears. This partisan outcome installs public sector nihilism and parental-rights-as-governance where the purpose of public education and participatory citizenship for government that works used to be.

To promote this outcome, partisans contend that public school governance rides roughshod over the rights due to parents/caregivers. Partisans paint a picture of malevolent public school governance where "the most important decisions regarding a student's education are being made by school administrators behind closed doors and are increasingly influenced by political activists" (Lennox, 2021, para. 1).

Partisan control ensures the least government. Oversight of education through strict enforcement of partisanship principles secures the right of parents/caregivers to enact their closely held beliefs. Parental rights, framed by *freedom from* government, reject any segment of the public sector with the temerity to foster a relationship between individual interests and government interests.

Replacing government that works with partisanship-that-works, partisans foster a social reality that prioritizes religious and ideological dictums. If partisans enact schooling in America, then any aspect of public education deemed burdensome by any parent/caregiver disappears like smoke in the wind.

SOCIAL EMOTIONAL LEARNING: A FEAR-INDUCING BOOGEYMAN

Protestant Christianity is a benchmark for partisanship. This comprehensive doctrine is integral to partisan education, partisan governance, and partisan social reality. This benchmark puts partisans in position to assert that their compelling interests are constitutionally protected.

Perhaps because this benchmark is so compelling, partisans assume that public educators are devoted to their own closely held beliefs that stand in direct opposition to what is right and what is true. The likelihood that this assumption propels partisan enmity is suggested by the fervor with which proponents of partisan education contend that traditional public schools brainwash students with a non-partisan comprehensive doctrine: social emotional learning (SEL).

SEL, from the point of view of partisans, interferes with the comprehensive doctrines of families, usurps the rights of parents, and interferes with students' mental health.

But research indicates that this aspect of instruction in public schools is misrepresented through consumer relations to facilitate partisan angst and to further justify the imposition of the compelling interests of partisanship throughout public education.

The Center for Reinventing Public Education reported that "SEL typically focuses on all students, while mental health interventions focus on students struggling with specific issues" (Chu and DeArmond, 2021, para. 2). Moreover, SEL often is treated as a sidecar on classroom instruction resulting in less than effective implementation. In fact, proponents urge that SEL should become more integral to classroom instruction (Sugishita and Dresser, 2019).

SEL is part of classroom practice to allow the purpose of traditional public education to corporate social-emotional development. *How to think*, by its very nature, incorporates SEL which is a vast set of "competencies and skills that support student success in school and in life including persistence, self-awareness, skillful communication and collaboration with peers, and self-regulation" (Chu and Armond, 2021, para. 2).

SEL engages students with these skills and numerous other dispositions sought by business and industry that have been designated by the Collaborative for Academic, Social and Emotional Learning as twenty-first-century skills (Chu and Armond, 2021).

Instead of inculcating students with tenets of comprehensive doctrine, "SEL curriculum has been implemented in schools through district adoptions of program-based interventions targeting specific issues such as bullying, drug use, or school violence" (Sugishita and Dresser, 2019, p. 40). SEL instruction is student-centric, focused skills that allow students to deal with "emotional issues that can inhibit students' abilities to focus at school" (Kingkade and Hixenbaugh, 2021, para. 14).

SEL engages all students in learning "the skills, behaviors, and attitudes that people need to manage their personal, social, and cognitive behaviors" (Yoder, 2014, quoted in Sugishita and Dresser, 2019, p. 37).

Nevertheless, partisans castigate public educators for offering SEL and falsely connect SEL with critical race theory. The compelling interests of partisanship are advanced when partisans react as if critical race theory is a co-parenting-with-the-government comprehensive doctrine maneuvered into public schools inside the Trojan Horse of SEL (Kingkade and Hixenbaugh, 2021; Sewell, 2022).

THE UNHERALDED RESOURCE FOR PARTISANSHIP

Partisans have no interest in "others" except when "others" are an obstacle to the imposition of partisanship. To fend off "others," partisans turn to their resources—fear mongering, anarchic dissent, public dissonance—to distance themselves from nefarious public school content and to distance social reality from knowing along with others, reciprocity, justice for all, and participatory citizenship.

Additional resources available to partisans include the compelling interests of partisanship that already enjoy a prominent role in the social reality, faith community, and private/partisan educational landscape of contemporary America. But the resource of greatest value to partisanship is rarely mentioned. This unheralded resource is the extent to which partisans already have extensive opportunities to engage their children fully with the principles of partisanship.

The extent and impact of this resource is revealed in a comparison between the time students spend in school and the time spent out of school (Rebell, 2014).

Using an average of seven hours in each of 180 weekdays, a student is in school for 1,260 hours per year. In contrast, a student's weekday family hours (seventeen per day) during the school year total 3,060. This school year difference is not, however, a complete tally of the time available to students for lived experiences with their closely held beliefs.

During the 185 days per year that students are not in school (weekends, holidays, summer), family time (twenty-four hours/day) adds up to 4,440 hours.

In the span of a calendar year, then, students are exposed to ideas in public school for 1,260 hours. In the span of a calendar year, students benefit from the influence of family beliefs and expectations for 7,500 hours. Parents and caregivers have important, proper, and extensive opportunities to share comprehensive beliefs with their children that promote responsive behavior as a result.

However, partisans, as mentioned earlier, distrust learners almost as much as they distrust government schools. Partisans, it seems, do not trust students to enact the enduring meaning of comprehensive doctrine during encounters with everyday life in the outside world.

Despite a multitude of different schools that engage students with the compelling interests of partisanship and that engage students with learning on behalf of static-balance, mistrust drives the attempt to immerse public schools and social reality in closely held beliefs.

Partisan furor over faith-neutral public education suggests that partisans have less faith in students' commitment to closely held beliefs than public educators have in students' capacities to engage with the outside world and its challenges.

A COMEUPPANCE FOR PARTISANSHIP

In the absence of terms of social cooperation that reason finds acceptable, the compelling interests in partisan education abandon respect for others as equal members of society because these non-partisans adhere to different comprehensive doctrines (Neufeld and Davis, 2010). This substantive denial of reciprocity is not lost on non-partisan parents and caregivers.

When partisans control public education, knowing along with others for the common good ebbs. As a result, concerns flow from non-partisans who wonder on behalf of their children about "what level of control they [partisans] should be able to exert over their classmates" (Richman and Smith, 2022, para. 5).

When partisans undermine traditional public education, non-partisans see an invitation to engage in good dissent on behalf of pluralism and purpose. Partisan imposition of closely held beliefs on public schooling can inspire what amounts to a parental rights counter-revolution because "insofar as schools are institutions that are designed to meet the needs of society, citizens need to ensure that those needs are being met" (Stitzlein, 2015, p. 61).

Put another way, those who defend public education push back against partisan control. The extent of this counter-revolution grows as the public recognizes the danger in the demise of neutrality in public schools. The danger is clear because "such action may 'save' one's child from harm but [will] leave behind unsolved problems for other children to encounter" (Stitzlein, 2020, p. 367).

The public's overwhelming support for traditional public education stands in direct opposition to partisan education that imposes its comprehensive doctrine (Neufeld and Davis, 2010).

Shining a light on this counter-revolution as a response to the discriminatory and exclusionary ethos of partisanship, Rubin (2022) reports that a national survey found that more than 95 percent of Americans want public schools to teach about slavery and 85 percent want public schools to engage students with learning about racial inequality. "These practices are important indicators because they help prepare youth for life in a diverse democracy, [and] the public is broadly supportive of them" (Rubin, 2022, para. 6).

From this counter-revolution, even a school board populated by elected ideologues can face possible legal action after implementing restrictions, censorship, and mandates that stop students from receiving communicated speech. For instance, in 2023, parents/caregivers in a Florida school district joined forces with PEN America and Penguin Random House in a lawsuit demanding that the school district restore books that had been banned by the school board (Yurcaba, 2023).

Further legal peril awaits school boards if they refuse to comply with "a federal law that bans sex-based discrimination in schools" (Jimenez, 2022, p. 6A). Compliance with Title IX, the federal statute that prohibits discrimination on the basis of sex, is mandatory if traditional public schools are to receive federal funding. Nevertheless, some states have passed laws "stripping the rights of students who are transgender and nonbinary" (Jimenez, 2022, para. 1).

Seemingly forgotten by partisans is that once ideologues become school board members they become "the government" in the sense that they are its agents. Attempts at censorship and attempts to impose a comprehensive belief can face daunting legal challenges.

Partisans who become the government cannot escape the premise that "local school authorities may not require the utterance of a particular message, because such action 'pose[s] the inherent risk that the government seeks . . . to suppress unpopular ideas or information or manipulate the public debate through coercion rather than persuasion'" (Salzman, 2022, p. 1084).

Moreover, the particular message imposed by partisans can incite strong local opposition that echoes the value that most Americans see in their public schools. For instance, rural communities and rural school districts push back when they recognize that partisan education robs local schools of funding, well-qualified teachers, and bright futures for all students (Swensson, Lehman, and Ellis, 2021). It turns out that when partisans become agents of the government, their efforts to ban ideas, school practices, and literature are suppression of ideas and speech that are not a governmental right.

The mantra of low cost as a virtue of partisan education also hits a sour note when partisans demand funding equal to, or in excess of, per pupil costs at traditional public schools. The financial vacuum created for public schools by the implementation of closely held beliefs burdens non-partisans and deprives students, families, and communities of the futures associated with traditional public education.

Despite animosity from parents, caregivers, and communities directed at the consequences of partisan education, self-serving intentions and unfulfilled promises are sustained as partisanship imposes universal singularity. Partisans launch "Liberty" on behalf of their goal to establish both partisan education and "self" government. This symbiotic relationship is a closed system, the destination where partisanship flourishes.

PART V

US Education: Journey or Destination?

Chapter 14

The Compass Rose

Purpose

Defending open futures for all students, public educators engage students with learning as a journey. During this journey, all students engage with intellectual autonomy as an amalgam of capabilities for individual success within the common good on behalf of government that works.

On the other hand, partisan education has no reason to orient students in this way because universal singularity is a one-way street to the destination of closely held beliefs, adult best interests, and "self" government. The compass rose of traditional public education is meaningless. Partisan education eschews the unfixed social world, intellectual autonomy, and the navigation of precarious-balance.

Purpose facilitates learning as a journey in many possible directions.

THE JOURNEY OF CONSTITUTIONAL DEMOCRACY

In the United States, constitutional democracy is, in large measure, a function of participatory citizenship derived from informal and formal education. "A modern liberal democracy could not function without a minimal level of political and moral literacy such as the rights and responsibilities associated with citizenship" (Marples, 2014, p. 27).

Citizenship education engages all students with political and moral literacy. As this discussion indicates, traditional public education is the foundation from which participatory citizenship and the dialectic for precarious-balance yield government that works in constitutional democracy.

Although both partisans and proponents of traditional public education are likely to agree that "the institutions that comprise the basic structure are those that have a 'profound effect' on the lives of individuals" (Neufeld and Davis, 2010, p. 104), how each major perspective construes the role of the individual and the identity of the institutions that comprise the basic structure could not be more different.

The compass rose of traditional public education guides and expresses the state's compelling interest in sustaining, improving, and renewing society. Carried out through curriculum and instruction, purpose puts the decisions and actions required to navigate the precarious-balance of democracy into the hands of participating citizens. Abandoning the threat of multiple directions in an unfixed democracy, partisan education puts the decisions and actions that craft social reality into the hands of a self-assigned protective partisan class.

Citizenship oriented via the purpose of public education is the journey necessary and sufficient for government that works. Government that works is a bouillabaisse of citizen intelligence, commitment, and action created from a recipe that includes several key ingredients:

- Entrusting "government infrastructure to oversee the daily running of schools" (Stitzlein, 2020, p. 368);
- Engaging *the public* in a "limited and proceduralist account of democracy and the social contract" (Stitzlein, 2020, p. 368); and
- Embedding individual rights in the moral, legislative, and judicial tapestry that encompasses America's social reality and denying the exercise of compelling interests of government where they are not justified.

Citizens oriented by the purpose of public education accept the obligation of paying for equity as balance. Individuals exercise extensive rights guaranteed by government that works. At the same time, they pay the cost of this significant freedom when the rule of law validates the compelling interests of government even though some of those compelling interests will not be endorsed by all citizens.

This is precarious-balance navigated by citizens who understand that Liberty depends on a structure of society that prevents unlimited individual rights for some that deliberately impede the exercise or expression of rights by others. Traditional public education and citizenship education prepare future voters with learning required to protect the equitable exercise of individual rights (Salzman, 2022).

The argument made here, and throughout this discussion, is that the basic structure of constitutional democracy depends upon governing "those aspects of upbringing that concern education for future citizenship" (Neufeld and Davis, 2010, p. 105). This understanding launches civic respect as the journey that traditional public education and compelling interests of government take together.

THE JOURNEY OF CIVIC RESPECT

Public schools (e.g., instruction, curriculum, concerns for others) and civic respect are works in progress. Traveling side by side, public education and civic respect invoke the reciprocal nature of citizenship which teaches "adequate civic respect for others, as well as the other skills necessary for their future lives as free and equal citizens" (Neufeld and Davis, 2010, p. 201).

In this context, good dissent is an expression of recognition respect to defend and enact the skills, and accept the costs, necessary and sufficient for consent *among* the governed:

> Consenting to principles of justice and political policies in a diverse society will involve understanding that others are motivated by different ends, consent will involve reflecting critically and independently upon one's own conceptions of the good and upon others' as well. (Reich, 2002, p. 456)

Reflection about conceptions of the good oriented by the compass rose of public education takes individuals beyond natural thinking and beyond self-justification of closely held beliefs. Consenting citizenship is a product of knowing along with others, accounting for the different ends that motivate others, and the reciprocity of civic respect.

Consent among the governed is not obtained readily or easily. Problems, issues, concerns, disagreements, and controversies are integral to human interactions and thus require knowledge, skills, and dispositions that yield give-and-take consent required for government that works.

Reciprocity, what is owed to others, is a pillar of constitutional democracy. The reciprocity woven into relational respect permits interpersonal exchanges that bend toward justice for all instead of universal singularity that bends toward the dictatorship of singularity riveted to partisan orthodoxy.

THE JOURNEY OF CITIZENSHIP EDUCATION

From its beginnings in the 1830s, traditional public education engaged students with celebratory patriotism as the epitome of citizenship education. The value of celebratory patriotism notwithstanding, citizenship education better understood as an investment in and study of the principles, practices, and rights that government must afford equitably to all citizens whose active participation is a fundamental expression of patriotism.

A participating citizen employs intellectual autonomy to apply (1) the rule of law; (2) how government actions are, or are not, aligned with the rule of law; and (3) the rights, responsibilities, and obligations afforded to citizens in democracy.

Citizenship education ranges from the principles of democracy to how a bill becomes a law, from the principles in America's founding documents to the failures to live up to these principles, and from the obligations of citizens to the responsibilities of government. Citizenship education leads the way to participatory citizenship.

Citizenship education explores participatory citizenship as its own journey during which navigating the precarious-balance between individual rights and the compelling interests of government evolves. Exploration during this journey is focused on engaging students with the core of "participatory democracy [which] emphasizes citizens as actively working together to shape public institutions and policies" (Stitzlein, 2015, p. 58).

Participatory citizenship, as it is understood throughout this narrative, is premised on the notion that "public" is "a verb that encompasses the act of creating common worlds through solving problems together for mutual benefit and bringing together different viewpoints around shared concerns" (Stitzlein, 2015, p. 58). Public education puts learning at the forefront of solving problems of precarious-balance.

Where citizenship education constructs a "big tent" of rights and responsibilities, partisan education offers a confined space to which only partisans are admitted. The difference between these educational spaces is profound; learning to be a citizen in public schools is a public thing while learning from partisan things invokes *the public* as singularity.

Singularity as *the public* is as close to participatory citizenship as partisanship gets. Partisan education aids and abets the destination for learning history with blinders on. Legislation that excludes topics, conflicts, controversies, depredations, and inconsistencies from classroom discussion, educational resources, and the future voting decisions of students is the equivalent of educational blind man's bluff that guarantees winning only for those who deserve it.

The "we" of participatory citizenship and the "we" of intellectual autonomy are lost when the compass rose of traditional public education is tossed aside and replaced by deceptive half-truths and omissions in instruction anchored by partisan dictates about what is right and what is true.

Denied access to ideas, constructs, or events rejected by partisanship, students are tied to learning that abandons discernment, objectivity, and skepticism. Excluded from these and other skills that represent intellectual autonomy, students subjected to partisanship are not aware that they have no access to the multiple outcomes oriented by the compass rose of public schools including the freedom to learn, the right to engage in good dissent, and the capabilities required to engage with difficult knowledge.

Learning from the ethos of partisan education (e.g., competition, fear-mongering, and ideological mandates), students discover that singularity is a guarantee that self-aggrandizing is a fulfilling substitute for citizenship because it denies "others" access to the scarce rights cherished by partisans.

Under these conditions, partisan education highlights celebratory patriotism as history's rationale for the depredations referred to in this narrative as *exclusionary citizenship*. Exclusionary citizenship is the power of universal singularity to assign "others" to the status of second-class citizens.

Second-class citizens are integral to the intentions of partisans. Static-balance is the skewed social reality in which partisanship engineers a moral high ground comprised of self-evident truths. Celebratory patriotism and exclusionary citizenship are among the truths that require no justification when exclusion, discrimination, denial of rights, and closely held beliefs replace participatory citizenship.

The truths of partisanship embraced by *the public* cling to certainty. Certainty permits denial of connections that signify relational respect at the core of citizenship. Abandoning citizenship for the comfort zones of partisanship, the certainties of celebratory patriotism ignore the violence and hate that were anything but a celebration for those denied the rights of participatory citizenship throughout America's history.

The Effects of Citizenship Education

In traditional public school classrooms, students grapple with the contradictions, activities, contributions, connections, problems, benefits, definitions, and events integral to navigating the history of precarious-balance that is a feature of constitutional democracy and contemporary social reality.

Citizenship education is integral to the purpose of public education. State constitutions speak to the obligation of government to provide education as a reciprocity that benefits both society and individuals. Framed as a positive right, public education is the source of multiple outcomes associated with the common good emerge, including:

- Bringing "diverse children together so they may respectfully engage each other in the practice of public reason" (Callan, 1997, quoted in Curren, 2009, p. 49);
- "Nurturing friendships that shrink the cultural chasms that divide society" (Curren, 2009, p. 49); and
- "Securing the social basis for a legitimate scheme of cooperation across generations" (Curren, 2009, p. 49).

These outcomes symbolize the common good realized when the positive frame "of education as a *social* right assign[s] society and its government an obligation to provide the child with an education" (Curren, 2009, p. 48, emphasis in original). Oriented via the compass rose of purpose, this obligation is the beginning of a journey toward intellectual autonomy, public reason, and legitimate schemes of cooperation.

Necessary Neutrality

The vast array of comprehensive doctrines held closely by families and individuals throughout America are studied in public schools. But public education does not prioritize any one of these doctrines. Teaching and learning any one comprehensive doctrine is the province and responsibility of entities outside the school house walls.

Correctly constituted as the closely held beliefs of families, faith-based organizations, and houses of worship, comprehensive doctrines are not situated within the purpose of traditional public schools and are not a feature of citizenship education. Separation of church and state is one of the myriad contested issues that, over time, represents the evolving navigation of precarious-balance.

Partisan education owns the premise that one faith is education to be imposed on all students. Indivisibility of church and state is a priority; faith-neutrality in education is unthinkable. For partisans, what is right and what is true is indistinguishable from the blend of one faith and celebratory patriotism fostered in partisan education. Turning a blind eye to pluralism, partisan education galvanizes static-balance to social reality and shuts the metaphorical door on a positive frame around the freedom to learn.

Balance as Equity

Citizenship education is the foundation for a give-and-take relationship between individuals and government. Instead of partisanship coercing "others" to accept the acquisitive determinants of a social reality crafted by transactional relationships, the purpose of traditional public education is the springboard for *balance as equity*.

Balance as equity is the evolving, teeter-totter-like equilibrium of social reality in which robust individual rights are nurtured by and respond to the government's compelling interests (e.g., paying taxes, licensing cars, conforming to health/safety mandates). Expressed another way, balance as equity entails individuals acting as citizens, even while dissenting, to "keep the focus on balancing individual freedoms with community goods, because citizens have a responsibility to do so" (Stitzlein, 2015, p. 68).

THE JOURNEY OF OPEN FUTURES

From a public educator's point of view, teaching and learning that fulfill the purpose of traditional public education are devoted to "a child's right to an open future" (Marples, 2014, p. 28). Participatory citizenship in a government that works requires nothing less.

Traditional public education is part of the social structure designed with the characteristics and components necessary and sufficient for every student to journey into an open future:

- Public education is carried out to realize a purpose that promotes the greater good for students and US democracy.
- Traditional public schools welcome all students and offer a multitude of programs, courses, and activities to engage them with learning.
- Citizenship education offered in public schools explores both historic successes and failures of the nation to help future voters perceive that citizenship suffused with balance as equity incorporates good dissent and improves constitutional democracy.
- Public educators abide by judicial rulings that ensure that public schools are a haven for students no matter their race, gender identity, special education needs, first language status, religion, or national origin/immigration status.

Well-prepared learners emerge as citizens, capable adults whose thinking and dispositions (e.g., resilience, concern about others, self-confidence, motivation) support government that works and the breadth of the public sector required for economic vitality, participatory citizenship, and freedoms safeguarded through constitutional democracy.

THE JOURNEY OF "WE" IN THE COMMON GOOD

How to think on behalf of the common good involves forming, considering, debating, valuing, and acting upon multiple points of view, deciphering a torrent of information, making sense of complicated interactions, and ethical meaning-making amid constant change.

Students will be involved with these, and many other, interactions in the "real world" as adults. Making sense of how precarious-balance is endemic to the outside world occurs when the relationship between individual advantage and the common good supports the cognition and behavior of "we." Participatory citizenship requires and sustains "we."

Every student's interplay of intelligences (i.e., practical, creative, emotional, analytic), developing initially as natural thinking, comes to school. This interplay in traditional public schools, expressed metaphorically as a double helix accessed during *dynamic instruction*, represents a public educator's intellectual autonomy employed to expand upon and respond to the intelligences of all students (Swensson and Shaffer, 2020).

Dynamic instruction is a resource that grows and improves students' engagement with ideas, challenges, conflicts, goals, problems, and diversity in the outside world. "We" emerges from this engagement so that adults (formerly students) become the foundation for government that works.

This is the learner-to-voter transformation fostered by *how to think*. Learners acquire public reason and public liberty (Fraser-Burgess, 2012) which allow teaching and learning "to operate independently of particular comprehensive doctrines" (Neufeld and Davis, 2010, p. 98).

Chapter 15

To Defend Public Education— Good Dissent

Anarchic dissent, as this discussion indicates, is deployed to undermine the purpose of traditional public education and to terminate the practices that support this purpose. Anarchic dissent and the lingering turmoil of public dissonance upend public schooling. Traditional public education appears to be at the mercy of its foes.

It's a mistake, however, to think that traditional public education has no resources with which to counteract intentions to disengage students from the capacities required to navigate precarious-balance. It's also a mistake to think that proponents of public schools have no way to defend against the resources, exclusive rights, and ethos of partisanship.

Of significance in a constitutional democracy, of value to participatory citizenship, and of meaning for the future for navigating precarious-dissonance is *good dissent*. Good dissent constitutes a substantial means of defending the purpose, practices, and outcomes of traditional public education (Stitzlein, 2020).

Good dissent is both simple and complex. Simply put, "good dissenters know when to compromise on their stands, when to alter them in light of new information, and when to hold them strongly—though not fixed once and for all" (Stitzlein, 2020, p. 361). Good dissent is an act of citizenship imbued with reciprocity, concerns for others, rights received, costs paid, and intellectual autonomy necessary and sufficient for government that works.

This is the complexity of good dissent; individuals "acting as citizens to the extent that they begin with shared concerns for others" (Stitzlein, 2020, p. 360). Good dissent is behavior that facilitates and accommodates the complexities and costs of enacting the common good.

Good dissent promotes the evolving mutuality between intellectual autonomy and individual rights sufficient to accept the cost of government that works for the common good. The common good is not only the acknowledgment of others' individual rights but is also the agreement that the compelling interests of government can modify or curtail some rights in the furtherance of balance as equity.

Beginning with a foundation of the common good as shared concerns for others, good dissent on behalf of traditional public education is how Americans "*ought* to act to best fulfill their responsibilities as citizens and to practice democracy on the behalf of children and schools" (Stitzlein, 2020, p. 356, emphasis in original).

When universal singularity—found throughout US history in the clash between partisanship (of one kind or another) and the common good—upends practices that foster shared concerns for others, good dissent serves as a counter-measure.

GOOD DISSENT AND PUBLIC THINGS

Traditional public education is a public thing. A public thing, as indicated earlier in this discussion, is a shared and intractable part of democratic life. As a public thing, traditional public education, through its purpose, engages all students with the capabilities for participatory citizenship. Shared and intractable, participatory citizenship gives life to democracy in the form of government that works by assessing and reassessing how to navigate the precarious-balance of public things on behalf of the common, shared good.

"Making things public does not resolve conflict but offers a way to see how various versions of 'we' are imperfectly but consistently constituted through public things realized through public work and educational decision-making at different levels of governance" (Knight Abowitz, 2018, p. 3). The "we" of constitutional democracy cannot happen unless challenges, conflicts, controversies, and disagreements are navigated and, however imperfectly, precariously balanced. Partisanship is undermined as this journey proceeds.

For this reason, good dissent is a public thing. The capabilities for good dissent acquired in public school classrooms are among the many building blocks of participatory citizenship. Reciprocity, negotiation, collaboration, disagreement, compromise, and shared concerns for others are among the capabilities for good dissent necessary for government that works. The very nature of government that works is intractable—persistently subject to change and difficult to control.

For partisans, good dissent is an existential dilemma. By definition, good dissent does not guarantee winning for the few who deserve it. Good dissent is problematic because partisan education rejects knowing along with others. Good dissent is meaningless because universal singularity rejects the relationships of reciprocity. Good dissent, as a public thing, is the antithesis of static-balance.

Believing that good dissent is meaningless, partisans reject the public sector and reject the need to navigate precarious-balance between individual rights and a working government. Good dissent cannot exist and does not work when partisanship is the name of an ethos—in education and for social reality—whose only outcome is winner-take-all (Swensson, Lehman, and Ellis, 2021).

Good dissent invites and accommodates instances of precarious-balance and expresses the capabilities of citizenship required to navigate instances of precarious-balance. The ethos of partisanship does not accommodate good dissent undertaken in the name of reciprocity and the common good.

Partisans use competition and anarchic dissent to disconnect public things from the common good. When disconnected from shared concerns for others, good dissent becomes inert. The self-serving pursuit of universal singularity crafts static-balance as the foundation of social reality. Anarchic dissent is the partisan firebrand that incinerates good dissent in the name of rights and partisan things sold only to the few.

THE ROLE OF GOOD DISSENT IS THE ROLE OF PUBLIC EDUCATION

The role of traditional public education in US democracy is to engage all students with understanding that navigating precarious-balance in America's social reality is "not just one citizen fighting for his or her own self-interest, but rather as a group of citizens working together to ensure the well-being of themselves and others, as well as democracy as a whole" (Stitzlein, 2020, p. 357). The role of good dissent and the role of public education are simultaneous and, as such, become the means for Liberty that allows for, but does not kowtow to, the impositions of partisanship.

Good dissent is at work when parents, caregivers, educators, and citizens push back against the imposition of partisanship priorities in public schools (LaGrone, 2023). Voters sharing the detrimental effects of ideology-driven education with elected officials enact good dissent as a feature of government that works.

For instance, patrons of one Florida school district decried the attempt by the school board president to hire a consultant affiliated with a private Christian college and feared that this affiliation made "him unqualified to examine district policies without bias" (LaGrone, 2023, para. 7). In the aftermath of a rally and public commentary against hiring the consultant, the school board voted not to make the hire.

Good dissent invokes the capabilities crafted for learners by the purpose of public education in the fulfillment of citizenship behaviors that influence and navigate the reciprocity of government that works (Stitzlein, 2020).

Traditional public education ought to be the state's endorsement—via legislation, funding, statute, and rule—of the power of public things to generate reciprocal responses to the compelling interests of government. "We" is this reciprocity between individual liberties and the government's exercise of its compelling interests. "We" becomes a statement made when voters participate in the processes that hold partisanship in check and, thus, validate equity as a baseline for constitutional democracy.

"We" is the synergy of teaching and learning in traditional public education that establishes the relationship between participatory citizenship and good dissent. "We educate so as to enable the student to *create* her or his future, not to submit to it" (Gunzenhauser and Hyde, 2007, p. 506, emphasis in original).

Defending traditional public education and sustaining its purpose are opportunities tailor-made for good dissent. When partisan control of school governance terminates ideological- and faith-neutrality, good dissent serves to thwart these malign objectives.

PART VI
Across the Great Divide

Chapter 16

The Chasm

This discussion began with a prediction and a teeter-totter. Sikkink (1999) identified the effect of a structural split between closely held beliefs and the purpose of traditional public education and intimated the future effect of this split. The teeter-totter was invoked as a metaphor about balance. Between the prediction and the metaphor lies the meaning of US education and the choices that will deliver one meaning or another to America's children and young people in the twenty-first century.

The prediction identified a small fissure across social reality that, decades later, has become a chasm. The metaphor turned out to be a picture of how each major perspective about education seeks balance despite the expanding chasm. Education will be either a bridge across this great divide or an earthquake destined to widen the gap. A bridge or an earthquake, the future of US education will emerge on one end or the other of several continuums including: "self" government and self-government, static-balance and precarious-balance, and universal singularity and government that works.

"SELF" GOVERNMENT OR SELF-GOVERNMENT

"Self" government is the least government possible. "Self" government is cobbled together in the wake of legislation designed to deconstruct government that works. "Self" government is an ideological construct designed to enforce static-balance. "Self" government exists after legislation installs the exclusive rights of partisanship that, when exercised, erode the rights of "others."

"Self" government is the amalgam of closely held beliefs whose purpose is to advantage partisans so that *learning along with others* becomes oxymoronic. The "self" in "self" government inflicts damage on the rights of non-partisans and on the ideological- and faith-neutrality central to public education and constitutional democracy. In the ethos of partisanship, "self" is the ultimate expression of "Liberty."

"Liberty" eschews the rule of law and the applicability of constitutional guarantees to non-partisans. "Self" government, in essence, is perpetual anarchic dissent.

Self-government, on the other hand, is the social structure and elements of the public sector through which citizens engage intellectual autonomy to navigate the precarious-balance of constitutional democracy.

Teaching and learning in traditional public education juxtapose freedom, diversity, majority rule, rights, costs, conflict, unity, tensions, the rule of law, and compelling interests of the state to engage all students with the capacities to engage in self-government from an understanding that self-government is intractable.

Accommodating intractability, a function of navigating precarious-balance, supporters of traditional public education turn to the rule of law as a shield against partisanship. The Supreme Court has affirmed a *government speech doctrine*. To function, the government can "express the views that it wants to express" and, in so doing, the government does not interfere with or curtail the speech of those who may disagree (Bowie, 2019, 33).

Curriculum and instruction in traditional public schools, thus, is not only government speech but, by its existence, is not interference with or a burden upon partisanship. Partisan claims that this government speech indoctrinates students is either sabotage aimed at the purpose of public education or propaganda meant to frighten the public.

Either way, the government speech doctrine validates the right of public schools to "speak" without constituting a burden and without any coercion directed at any belief, cohort of citizens, or ideological premise.

There is a "flip side" to the government speech doctrine. Not only is government speech not an infringement on partisanship but partisanship is subject to the relationship between rights and the compelling interests of government. As Bowie indicates, the Supreme Court interpreted the First Amendment by "applying the government-could-not-work doctrine whenever uninhibited speech or religious exercise would undermine political or religious pluralism or society's ability to self-govern" (2019, p. 39).

Constitutional democracy could not work if learning for citizenship in a pluralistic society erodes under a torrent of partisanship. Such a flood would constitute uninhibited speech or religious exercise. Pluralism at the core of traditional public education and the neutrality embedded in the government speech of public schools are shielded; government schools could not work if a tsunami of closely held beliefs swept them away.

Nevertheless, partisanship asserts that individual rights take precedence without regard for the compelling interests or function of government and without regard for the closely held beliefs or rights of non-partisans. Partisanship undermines pluralism and the common good whereby society's ability to self-govern is stymied. Partisan education is the denial of both pluralism and its democratic ideal when ideologues overtake public school governance.

STATIC-BALANCE OR PRECARIOUS-BALANCE

Static-balance is the goal of partisan education; navigating precarious-balance is the goal of the purpose of traditional public education. How students are educated to meet these goals spawns the relationship between social reality and either government that works or universal singularity. For the sake of static-balance, partisanship compels student conduct.

Static-balance is the epitome of control, a central objective of those who impose closely held beliefs. Control is critical because intellectual autonomy is perceived as a platform from which students may challenge the lifeworld of static-balance. Exposure to ideas, the universe of discourse, and open futures constitute a journey partisanship will not take because the journey leads away from the destination of partisan education.

Exposure to the universe of discourse in traditional public schools equips students with the capacities for navigating the precarious-balance of government that works is a threat to static-balance. Teaching and learning that support government that works are a burden upon partisan claims of exclusivity. Exclusivity, limitation, and orthodoxy symbolize the partisan imperative to undermine the rule of law.

Partisan antipathy toward government that works and the partisan belief that government is ipso facto intrusive cannot obscure that the rule law protects freedom of religion for all individuals. Government speech, thus, must be neutral in this regard.

The balance prompted by the rule of law is illuminated in an example of justice enacted while navigating precarious-balance. The Supreme Court ruled that "while a student may sometimes be 'forced to speak or write on a particular topic even though the student might prefer a different topic,' public schools 'may not demand that a student profess beliefs or views with which the student does not agree'" (Salzman, 2022, pp. 1083–84).

This illustration confirms that reciprocity is the exercise of equity when government that works crafts decisions on behalf of the common good. Partisan fury over invented governmental intrusion does not withstand the equity of the rule of law as it is derived from knowing along with others.

Nevertheless, partisans do not trust any entity in the public sector created under the aegis of self-government that, when navigating precarious-balance, cannot, does not, and will not guarantee winning for those who deserve it. Precluding "others" from the rights guaranteed by allegiance to partisanship, static-balance is the secure location for a social reality oriented to "self" and universal singularity.

UNIVERSAL SINGULARITY OR GOVERNMENT THAT WORKS

As Bowie indicates, the Supreme Court has interpreted the First Amendment by "applying the government-could-not-work doctrine whenever uninhibited speech or religious exercise would undermine political or religious pluralism or society's ability to self-govern" (2019, p. 39).

Universal singularity is the commitment to uninhibited "self" dedicated to the premise that government should not work. Unlimited rights sold in the marketplace and available only to partisans give universal singularity a cachet unavailable from government that works. Restrictions, reciprocity, and the republican principle do not apply to those devoted to the monocular vision of partisanship.

Government that works, on the other hand, is a panoramic vision of the complexities inherent in human behavior, in precarious-balance, and in concerns for others. Constitutional democracy, a perpetual work in progress, requires envisioning a kaleidoscopic and evolving social reality. The dynamic of change, the human propensity for innovation, the historic nature of the drive to improve—all emerge when the journey of traditional public education empowers participatory citizenship for government that works.

Universal singularity is an anchor; government that works is a sail. Universal singularity is the earthquake; government that works is the bridge. Partisanship thrives in the structural split; traditional public education heals a wounded social reality.

Chapter 17

Critical Questions

This discussion is a wide-ranging encounter with the influence of the structural divide on perspectives and issues critical to the future of US education. The chasm that now separates the two major perspectives about US education leads this narrative to critical questions. Answers to these questions will predict whether US education is to bridge the chasm or expand the divide.

The questions and their answers deal with fundamental differences that underlie how the future of teaching, learning, citizenship, and government will evolve. Three differences hold the key to predictions about education and social reality in the twenty-first century: the fixed and unfixed social world, the constraint and coercion of liberty, and the assumptions of education about justice.

QUESTION #1: IS SOCIAL REALITY FIXED OR UNFIXED?

Partisanship knows what's broken and will fix it: The extent to which social reality is broken is the extent to which it does not comport with closely held beliefs. In terms of US education, what's broken is teaching and learning that prepares all students to navigate precarious-balance throughout an unfixed social reality. To fix what's broken, partisans are duty bound to weld public education, government that works, and the outside world to the anchor of closely held beliefs.

A fixed social reality is woven from the certainties that frame what is right and what is true. What is right and what is true guide partisan education toward the destination of universal singularity. A fixed social reality is the preeminent destination within which the closely held beliefs of partisanship thrive. Partisans are tethered to inviolable, immutable, and absolute outcomes.

When, on the other hand, traditional public education recognizes equity as balance and "we" as concerns for others, an unfixed social world is social reality. Teaching and learning that facilitate the navigation of intractability are imperative for individual and societal success.

If partisanship is the choice of the future, control of a fixed social world is dictatorial, authoritarian, or chaotic because singularity and certainty must rule. In a fixed social world, "we" evaporates and "self" is social reality. The partisan fixation on locus of control guarantees "that education is a private possession, something we shop for as if it were a car" (Hinnefeld, 2023a, para. 5). The intention of partisans is to drive US education as a private possession whenever and wherever they please.

If traditional public education is the choice of the future, an unfixed social world is navigated via intellectual autonomy to facilitate meaning-making on behalf of reciprocity in the common good. Under these circumstances, control is established in the rule of law; the arbitrary use of power is subordinated to the exercise of well-defined statutes.

Government that works for an unfixed social world responds to the ultimate precarious-balance: the tension between diversity and unity. This means that social reality is mutable, responsive, intractable, and evolving. Government that works monitors, legislates, and adjudicates this precarious-balance when voters exercise participatory citizenship initiated in response to learning aligned with the purpose of traditional public education.

The leverage provided to individuals and society by traditional public education incorporates the ability to respond to change, the ability to advocate, the ability to want improvement, the ability to acknowledge the worth of others, and the ability to compromise. Always able to navigate, citizens educated in public school classrooms travel beyond partisanship while acknowledging this destination as one element among many that necessitate determining best interests amid precarious-balance.

QUESTION #2: IS LIBERTY CONSTRAINT OR COERCION?

The importance of this question lies in the nature of unfixed social reality and its evolving, and precarious, balance. Liberty is both constraint and coercion. The gist of educational choice, then, comes down to which liberty, which rationale for constraint and coercion, is acceptable when the social reality invoked by partisan education or traditional public education splits.

Both constraint and coercion accompany the false consciousness that gives permission for unfettered, unlimited, self-aggrandizing human behavior. "Liberty" is the label that partisans assign to the imposition of this aggregation of unlimited individual rights. Unlimited individual rights for the partisan few, however, are nothing less than the constraint of liberty for "others" and the coercion of "others" to adopt or conform to "Liberty."

Constraint of "others" is an essential characteristic of "Liberty" because partisanship depends on exclusion to ensure that the scarce benefits of closely held beliefs are rationed efficiently. Anarchic dissent and public dissonance are the tools of coercion that belie the otherwise benign meaning of "Liberty."

"Liberty" is proclaimed as if it guarantees the freedom for all, the equity, associated with the founding principles of the United States. "Liberty," however, is a partisan bait and switch. Offering "Liberty," and then replacing it with constraint and coercion, prevents access by too many to the self-assigned rights squirreled away by and for partisans.

Liberty, on the other hand, suffuses learning *how to think* on behalf of the common good and empowers students to navigate the precarious-balance of social reality, government that works, and justice for all. The tools of conscience (e.g., collaboration, compromise, civic respect) build reciprocity necessary and sufficient for citizens to coexist with the compelling interests of government.

In this give and take lies the constraint and coercion inherent in the relationships crafted via participatory citizenship. "For any government to function—especially in a politically and religiously pluralistic society like the United States—it must be able to compel residents to do all sorts of things a minority might disagree with" (Bowie, 2019, p. 5).

Because government that works entails individual costs paid for Liberty of the common good, the government obligation to act is coercive on its face; although, of course, such action may constitute restraint of unbridled partisanship to protect reciprocity, equity, and concerns for others.

Even those who might begrudge Liberty for government that works recognize how the admixture of constraint and coercion facilitates a give and take between individual rights and the compelling interests of government. Supreme Court Justice Antonin Scalia wrote: "However much we might wish that it were otherwise, government simply could not operate if it were required to satisfy every citizen's religious needs and desires" (Bowie, 2019, p. 28).

Self-government and "self" government are different combinations for constraint and coercion that either permit the purpose of traditional public education or attenuate the public sector from partisan education in favor of universal singularity.

The notion of Liberty that emerges from teaching and learning in public education is equitable in the same sense that artistic representations of Justice wear a blindfold. Liberty does not privilege or preference any cohort of the population, any one comprehensive doctrine, or any dictatorial/authoritarian premise. Traditional public education prompts Liberty in the exercise of the rule of law and majority rule.

Constraint and Coercion in Partisan Education

When partisanship envisions a fixed social world, social reality is an amalgam of constraints that take hold in education:

- Discussion topics in public school classrooms are curtailed.
- Books deemed "harmful" to the ethos of the fixed social world are banned.
- Public school governance is an exercise in denial and restriction.
- Legislation is promulgated to criminalize educators and librarians who make "uncomfortable" books available to students.

When "Liberty" is both constraint and coercion, the intent is to confine the public sector to the preferences, dictates, and priorities of partisanship. Bending "others" to these proclivities, partisans ensure that barriers or threats to closely held beliefs are removed from social reality. Putting constraint and coercion in the service of orthodoxy for education ensures that partisans perpetuate static-balance that separates and excludes.

Constraint and coercion sustain a fragmented social reality in which partisans enjoy and manipulate the distance apart from non-partisans created by "Liberty." Denied the right to shop for partisan education, non-partisans are denied access to the marketplace as the destination that supplies privilege.

"Liberty" is the embrace of boutique-ideology, the ideological boundaries past which teaching and learning cannot go to ensure partisan education fosters a definitive lifeworld and system. Partisan education is replete with the certainties that sustain the constraint and coercion required for partisanship to function.

For partisans, certainties are expectations; for non-partisans, certainties are restrictions and exclusions that define the destination of static-balance. "Self" government is the certainty that unlimited individual rights justify the imposition of closely held beliefs meant to ensure that "others," the public sector, and the rule of law are ineffective barriers to universal singularity.

Court findings that exposure does not constitute compulsion to believe or behave contrary to the lifeworld of partisanship are ignored when self-evident truths confirm the coercive nature of government and public education (Reich, 2002). Claiming that traditional public education's neutral stance is indoctrination or brainwashing, partisans deflect attention from Liberty and focus on unswerving inculcation of closely held beliefs.

"Partisan taint" is the *raison d'etre* of partisan education. Students are expected to learn the ways of thinking unique to and validated by partisanship. For instance, the mission of the Free to Learn Coalition "is to support parents, caregivers, and grassroots community organizations fighting to rid their schools of political content and to refocus on core skills" (Lennox, 2021, para. 1).

Constraint and Coercion in Traditional Public Education

Constraint and coercion are endemic to traditional public education because both are essential for Liberty. Liberty, as this discussion illustrates, is the expression of reciprocity and concern for others that invokes constraint and coercion. Reciprocity constrains unlimited individual rights. Concerns for others coerce my-side bias and reflexive self-aggrandizement.

As discussed earlier, traditional public education invokes citizenship education as the understanding that both constraint and coercion are necessary for Liberty. This is the acknowledgment of trade-offs in social reality that maximize rights for all citizens while prohibiting the rights of some citizens to supersede the rights of other citizens.

Traditional public education, through its purpose, constrains and coerces partisanship. Open futures for all students, facilitated by teaching and learning devoted to intellectual autonomy, erode the partisan premise that only static-balance and closely held beliefs are worthy determinants of social reality.

Put another way, public schools provide all students with the navigation skills required to make up their own minds and these capabilities are anathema to the lifeworld and social reality sought via partisanship.

How to think on behalf of the common good, intellectual autonomy is coercive. The open futures facilitated through intellectual autonomy, for partisans, are coercive because "autonomy means providing an environment where choice is meaningful, where opportunities to lead one kind of life or another are real options" (Reich, 2002, p. 456). Meaningful choice to navigate precarious-balance is the resource and capability shared in every public school classroom to permit participatory citizenship that bends the arc of the moral universe toward justice.

QUESTION #3: DOES EDUCATION ASSUME A VALUE OF JUSTICE?

Justice is a quality of fairness. Justice is equitable. Justice is the administration of the rule of law in pursuit of fairness and equity. Justice is genuine respect for all people.

At the core of this discussion is the assumption that justice develops from learning the intentions of fair social cooperation enacted during the relationship between traditional public education, citizenship education, participatory citizenship, and constitutional democracy for government that works.

As Neufeld and Davis indicate, the basic structure of society incorporates institutions that satisfy "the criterion of reciprocity in their public social relations with each other" (2010, p. 106). This egalitarian representation of justice emerges as one outcome of the journey oriented by the compass rose of traditional public education.

However, from a partisan perspective, justice is encased in static-balance maintained when the closely held beliefs of partisanship surround social reality. Justice is served, under these conditions, when self-proclaimed rights and a self-serving ethos guarantee universal singularity.

For partisans, justice is found in a social reality and in an educational system that espouses the *consistent practice* and *sustained faith* necessary to the continuity of the community of partisanship. The community of partisanship is like a constellation. Partisans are singular, but linked, when an ideological fence and closely held beliefs shape their preferred destination.

Partisanship is an ideological commitment to self-aggrandizement as justice. Delivering justice to themselves, partisans establish their perspective as the right due to their status as "a situated group of people within society" (Brantmeier, 2007, pp. 2–3).

The future of the great divide will be determined when either connection or separation control US education. Choosing between traditional public education and partisan education will validate, or invalidate, the observation that

> the state is responsible for ensuring that all children receive an education adequate for them to be free and equal citizens, capable of interacting with other citizens on the basis of civic respect, whereas parents are free to raise their children in accordance with their "comprehensive" religious, moral, and philosophical views. (Neufeld and Davis, 2010, p. 95)

Imposition of "Liberty," comprehensive doctrine, closely held beliefs, and static-balance activates control of the resources and mechanisms required to invoke partisanship as cultural determination. If there is a sense of "we" associated with partisanship, it is this sense of singularity that establishes "self" as a special class. This subversion of knowing along with others permits partisans to shop for a bowdlerized sense of "we." "Self" replaces "we" when partisanship drains the common good from social reality.

If partisanship's infatuation with "self" defines social reality, then "we" that sustains government that works, traditional public education, and navigating precarious-balance is lost.

Defending public education, "we" expresses the role of Liberty for cultural self-determination engaged during instruction in traditional public education. Learning, in this way, is control; the purpose of public education puts all students in position for meaning-making sufficient for egalitarian cultural self-determination. Government that works through the rule of law emerges from the capacities of adults/voters who navigate a precarious social reality.

"We" is the inclusion of others; "self" is the denial of "we."

Will America's future education come under the control of the comprehensive doctrine in partisanship? Will, on the other hand, America's future education incorporate *how to think* on behalf of the common good to engage all students with reciprocity and civic respect required for participatory citizenship?

The extent to which either major perspective represents coercion in the future for learning can be considered in light of Supreme Court Justice Blackmun's concurrence with the *Pico* ruling. Justice Blackmun confirmed that it's critical for students to receive ideas communicated in public school without "partisan taint."

The Justice opined that "'students may not be regarded as closed-circuit recipients of only that which the State chooses to communicate.' To allow otherwise would risk turning 'state-operated schools' into 'enclaves of totalitarianism'" (Salzman, 2022, pp. 1081–82).

Allowing otherwise is not a risk associated with the ideological- and faith-neutrality of the purpose of traditional public education. Intellectual autonomy and open futures at the core of the purpose of public schools provide students with the capabilities to thwart any such enclave.

But the insistent ideological and one-faith baseline of partisan education is its own enclave. Public education eschews state-endorsed and promulgated "partisan taint." Traditional public education, also, eschews partisanship and the dictatorial enclave of closely held beliefs imposed when partisan education taints learning with static-balance. Public education is the journey of Liberty because it "requires not only a commitment to a set of principles but some form of appropriate attachment to one's fellow citizens" (Stitzlein, 2020, p. 370).

The power of public schooling, as Tang illustrates, is a statement about the goals of traditional public education: "To build and sustain democracy, to teach young people how to live and work together with others, and to teach the skills and knowledge needed to participate fully in society" (2018, p. 358). Knowing along with others and concern for others represent a reciprocity that connects and benefits citizenship; the majority of citizens are served when cultural self-determination is the flourishing of diversity.

Conscience, knowing along with others, leverages social reality and the basic structure of society to align teaching and learning with equity and justice at the heart of constitutional democracy. Spurred by knowing along with others, "society's concern with . . . [children's] . . . education lies in their role as future citizens, and so in such essential things as their acquiring the capacity to understand public culture and to participate in its institutions, [and] in their being economically independent and self-supporting members of society over a complete life" (Neufeld and Davis, 2010, p. 102).

This expression of structure for the common good incorporates an understanding of the necessity to navigate precarious-balance to ameliorate the split structure of society. Traditional public education, in its reliance on knowing along with others, puts student-centric teaching at the center of learning that builds the capacity for connections and the ability to navigate social reality.

Concern for others is inclusionary, autonomous, and emphatically public.

The overriding rationale for Liberty as a catalyst in the equation of knowing along with others lies in the realization that "the need to deal with contradictory perspectives will inevitably arise, and as a society we desperately need to begin approaching this plurality using the tools of critical analysis and constructive dialogue" (Hoggan and Kloubert, 2020, p. 304).

Government that works in constitutional democracy thrives when participatory citizenship evinces these capacities. Liberty is the core of student-centric education. "What is actually going on in many schools is an attempt to ensure that every student has an experience that elevates their opportunity, that validates their identity, that ensures engagement and curiosity" (Pendarkar, 2022, para. 2).

Liberty is synonymous with trust; in the presence of Liberty, each citizen is trusted with the right to choose and act as an integral part of the relationship with the compelling interests of government. Traditional public education endows all students with the capabilities of trust. From every public school classroom emerges the best defense for connections, equity, common concerns, reciprocity, justice, the power of participatory citizenship, and the intellectual autonomy necessary for the open futures that all of America's students deserve.

Epilogue

It is almost impossible to predict the future accurately. This discussion began with a rarity: a prescient insight into the split that now divides public education from partisanship and pits the common good against universal singularity. Balance, under these circumstances, is a teeter-totter's expression of the choices between navigating precarious-balance and adhering to static-balance.

This discussion illustrates the dangers presented by the ascendance of "self" government as a replacement for self-government, participatory citizenship, and the primary purpose of traditional public education. Partisanship expands the great divide and denies constitutional protections for all citizens whose beliefs do not align with the "chosen" closely held beliefs.

Learning, under these circumstances, is prefabricated thinking. Intelligence, then, is relegated to a tiny corner of the universe of discourse.

So many doors to learning are closed, so many pathways that lead into the universe of discourse are blocked; partisan education is nothing less than the limitations, restrictions, and fears that ideologues embrace.

Hoggan and Kloubert phrase the question that lingers in the wake of this discussion: "Should our pedagogical attention be placed on fostering the skills and habits that would promote more effective living in a pluralistic society, which include critical assessment of one's own perspective?" (2020, p. 304).

One of the major perspectives about US education began this discussion. The most fitting epilogue, then, would be a communication that represents the other major perspective: traditional public education. Each reader now has access to content and insights sufficient to write a prediction for the future of public education. Each reader, after all, will share responsibility for choosing between the purpose of traditional public education and universal singularity in response to the enduring divide within social reality.

The epilogue for this discussion, as a result, is now in the hands of each reader. An email that did not introduce this discussion is now open to incorporate your "take" on the future of America's schooling.

To: (insert name of educator or school)
Fr: (reader's name here)
RE: The Way Education Ought to Be
It was a genuine pleasure to tour Open Futures Middle School with you earlier today. With students totally engaged in active learning throughout the building, I wanted to remain in every classroom to hear the thinking and watch the collaboration in action. I'm very impressed by . . . (Reader: your prediction goes here . . .)

References

Ali, S. (2019). A Second-Class Workforce: How neoliberal policies and reforms undermined the educational profession. *Journal of Curriculum and Teaching, (8)*3, 102–10. doi:10.5430/jct.v8n3p102.

Arnett, P. (1968, February 8). Major describes move. *New York Times*.

Atterbury, A. (2022, November 30). DeSantis-backed school boards begin ousting Florida educators. *Politico*. https://politico.com/news/2022/11/30/desantis-school-board-covid-00071305.

Balingit, M. (2022, September 13). Wanted: Teachers. No training necessary. *The Washington Post*. https://www.washingtonpost.com/education/2022/09/13/teacher-requirements-shortage-jobs/.

Beck, C. (2022, October 27). Anti-CRT, other PACs back school board candidates. Here's why you should care. *The Indianapolis Star*. https://www.indystar.com/story/news/education/2022/10/27/election-2022-school-board-races-indiana-pac-spending-money/69571963007/.

Beck, C. (2023, May 7). "A feature of the system, not a bug," one third of Indy charter schools close. *The Indianapolis Star,* 1A, 11A–13A.

Bergner, D. (2022, September 6). Daring to speak up about race in a divided school district. *The New York Times*. https://www.nytimes.com/2022/09/06/magazine/leland-michigan-race-school.

Bindewald, B. J. (2015). In the world, but not of the world: Understanding conservative Christianity and its relationship with American public schools. *Educational Studies, (51)*2, 93–111. doi:10.1080/00131.2015.1015343.

Binkley, C., and J. Carr Smyth. (2022, October 11). Conservative PACs inject millions into local school races. *Associated Press*. https://apnews.com/article/entertainment-elections-education-school-boards-teaching-059f2465829ab009394469b95c8cc94a#.

Black, D. W. (2019, December). Educational gerrymandering: Money, motives, and constitutional rights. *New York University Law Review, (94)*6, 1385–464.

Board of Education v. Pico, 474 F. Supp. 387 (E.D.N.Y., 1979).

Bowie, N. (2019). The government-could-not-work doctrine. *Virginia Law Review, (105)*1, 1–61.

Brantmeier, E. J. (2007, Spring). "Speak our language . . . abide by our philosophy": Language & cultural assimilation at a U.S. Midwestern high school. *Forum on Public Policy, 2.*

Brown v. Board of Education, 347 US 483 (1954).

Burron, A. (1996). Parents' rights—society's imperatives: A balancing act. *Educational Leadership, (53)*7, 80–82.

Chu, L., and M. DeArmond. (2021). Report. Approaching SEL as a whole-school effort, not an add-on: Lessons from two charter networks. Center on Reinventing Public Education, University of Washington, Bothell.

Chubb, J. E., and T. M. Moe. (1990). *Politics, markets, and America's schools.* Washington, DC: The Brookings Institution.

Conway, D. M. (2022). The assault on critical race theory as pretext for populist backlash on higher education. *Saint Louis University Law Journal, (66)*4, 707–19. https://scholarship.law.slu.edu/lj/vol66/iss4/5.

Craig, T. (2021, October 16). Moms for Liberty taps "parental rights" as a rallying cry. *The Washington Post.* wapo.855a8866-2e06-11ec-985d-3150f7e106b2.

Cunningham, M. (2022, October 10). The right-wing money and influence behind Moms for Liberty. *Bucks County Beacon.* https://buckscountybeacon.com/2022/10/the-right-wing-money-and-influence-behind-moms-for-liberty/.

Curren, R. (2009). Education as a social right in a diverse society. *Journal of Philosophy of Education, (43)*1, 45–56. https://academic.oup.com/jope/article-abstract/43/1/45/6840936.

Dewey, J. (1916). *Democracy and education.* www.public-library.uk.

Dvorak, P. (2023, March 23). Parents' rights? How about a 'parents' bill of responsibilities' instead? *The Washington Post.* https://www.washingtonpost.com/dc-md-va/2023/03/23/parents-rights-bill-parents-responsibilities/.

Edsall, T. B. (2022, December 14). There's a reason there aren't enough teachers in America. Many reasons, actually. *The New York Times.* https://www.nytimes.com/2022/12/14/opinion/teacher-shortage-education.html.

Farmer, R. (2001). The school prayer issue. *Education, (104)*3, 248–49.

Fraser-Burgess, S. (2012). Group identity, deliberative democracy, and diversity in education. *Educational Philosophy and Theory, (44)*5, 480–501. doi: 10.1111/j.1469-5812.201000717.x.

Friedman, M. (1955). The role of government in education. In Robert A. Solo (Ed.), *Economics and the public interest,* 123–44. New Brunswick, NJ: Rutgers University Press. https://miltonfriedman.hoover.org/objects/58044//the-role-of-government-in-education.

Friedman, J. N. (2022, September 1). School is for social mobility. *The New York Times.* https://www.nytimes.com/2022/09/01/opinion/us-school-social-mobility.

Frost, R. (1942). *Collected poems of Robert Frost.* Garden City, NY: Halcyon House.

Golden, E. (2021, July 24). Minnesota school board members resigning in record numbers. *(Minneapolis) Star Tribune.* https://www.startribune.com/more-minnesota-school-board-members-resign-in-turbulent-year/600081113/.

Granger, D. A. (2008). No Child Left Behind and the spectacle of failing schools: The mythology of contemporary school reform. *Educational Studies, 43*, 206–28. doi:10.1080/00131940802117654.

Gunzenhauser, M. G., and A. M. Hyde. (2007). Book review. What is the value of public school accountability? *Educational Theory, (57)*4, 489–507.

Gutmann, A., and S. Ben-Porah. (2015). Democratic education. In Michael T. Gibbons (Ed.), *The encyclopedia of political thought*, 1–12. West Sussex, UK: John Wiley & Sons, Ltd.

Harris, E. A., and A. Alter. (2022, December 12). A fast-growing network of conservative groups is fueling a surge in book bans. *The New York Times.* https://www.nytimes.com/2022/12/12/books/book-bans-libraries.html.

Hartman, D. A. (2005). Constitutional responsibility to provide a system of free public schools: How relevant is the states' experience to shaping governmental obligations in emerging democracies? *Syracuse Journal of International Law and Commerce, 33*(95), 95–114.

Hartsfield, D. E., and S. C. Kimmel. (2020). Supporting the right to read: Principles for selecting children's books. *The Reading Teacher, (74)*4, 419–27. doi:10.1002/trtr.1954.

Herron, A. (2022, November 20). Conservative wave didn't wash over the suburbs. *The Indianapolis Star,* 1A, 9A.

Herron, A., and C. Beck. (2022, October 30). Focus of CRT fight turns to local races. *The Indianapolis Star,* 1A, 12A.

Hess, F. M. (2010). Does school choice "work"? *National Affairs,* Fall, 35–53. www.nationalaffairs.com/publications/detail/does-school-choice-work.

Hinnefeld, S. (2023a, January 12). Expanding voucher program would be bad for kids, band for Indiana. *Indiana Capital Chronicle.* https://indianacapitalchronicle.com/2023/01/12/expanding-voucher-program-would-be-bad-for-kids-bad-for-indiana/.

Hinnefeld, S. (2023b, May 1). Voucher expansion aids the rich. *School Matters.* https://inschoolmatters.wordpress.com/2023/05/01/voucher-expansion-aids-the-rich.

Hixenbaugh, M. (2022, August 25). How a far-right, Christian cellphone company "took over" four Texas school boards. *NBC News.* https://www.nbcnews.com/news/us-news/-christian-cell-company-patriot-mobile-took-four-texas-school-boards-rcna44583.

Hixenbaugh, M. (2023, March 21). Inside the rural Texas resistance to the GOP's private school choice plan. *NBC News.* https://www.nbcnews.com/news/us-news/rural-texas-resistance-gop-private-school-choice-voucher-rcna75775.

Hoggan, C., and Kloubert, T. (2020). Transformative learning in theory and practice. *Adult Education Quarterly, (70)*3, 295–307. doi:10.1177/0741713620918510.

Imoukhuede, A. A. (2019). Enforcing the right to public education. *Arkansas Law Review, 72*(2), 443–65.

Jenkins, J. D. (2021, October 20). I'm a Florida school board member. This is how protesters come after me. *The Washington Post.* https://www.washingtonpost.com/outlook/2021/10/20/jennifer-jenkins-brevard-school-board-masks-threats/.

Jimenez, K. (2022, October 23). Abortion bans, LGBTQ laws bring controversy at schools. *The Indianapolis Star,* 6A.

Kahlenberg, R. D., and H. Potter. (2014, August 30). The original charter school vision. *The New York Times.* https://www.nytimes.com/2014/08/31/opinion/sunday/albert-shanker-the-original-charter-school-visionary.html.

Kingkade, T., and M. Hixenbaugh. (2021, November 15). Parents protesting "critical race theory" identify another target: Mental health programs. *NBC News.* https://www.nbcnews.com/news/us-news/parents-protesting-critical-race-theory-identify-new-target-mental-hea-rcna4991.

Klicka, C. J., and D. W. Phillips. (1997, November). Why parental rights laws are necessary. *Educational Leadership, (55)*3, 80–83.

Knight Abowitz, K. (2018). The war on public education: Agonist democracy and the fight for schools as public things. *Philosophical Inquiry in Education, 25*(1), 1–15.

Kurtzleben, D. (2022, May 31). Progressives take a leaf out of the conservative playbook to target school boards. *NPR, Morning Edition.* https://www.npr.org/2022/05/31/1101399058/progressives-take-a-leaf-out-of-the-conservative-playbook-to-target-school-board#.

Labby, S., F. C. Lunenburg., and J. R. Slate. (2012). Emotional intelligence and academic success: A conceptual analysis for educational leaders. *International Journal of Educational Leadership Preparation, 7*(1), 1–11.

LaGrone, K. (2023, April 19). Sarasota school board votes against hiring consultant linked to Hillsdale College. *WFTS (Tampa Bay).* https://www.abcactionnews.com/news/region-sarasota-manatee/sarasota-school-board-votes-against-hiring-consultant-linked-to-hillsdale-college#.

Lee, J. (2018). Understanding site selection of for-profit educational management organization charter schools. *Education Policy Analysis Archives, (26)*77, 3–17. http://dx.doi.org/10/14507/epaa.26.3024.

Lehrer-Small, A. (2023, May 1). Texas guts "woke civics." Now kids can't engage in a key democratic process. *The Guardian.* https://www.theguardian.com.

Lennox, S. (2021). "Free to Learn" coalition exposes the politicization of K-12 schools in brutal ad campaign. *PJMedia.* https://pjmedia.com/news-and-politics/stacey-lennox/2021/06/26/free-to-learn-exposes-k-12-schools-using-politicized-curriculum-in-brutal-ad-campaign-n1457412.

Levin, H. M. (2002). A comprehensive framework for evaluating educational vouchers. *Educational Evaluation and Policy Analysis, (24)*3, 159–74. https://www.jstor.org/stable/3594163.

Lewis, J. (2012). *Across that bridge: Life lessons and a vision for change.* New York: Legacy Lit.

Little, O. (2021, November 12). Unmasking Moms for Liberty. *Media Matters for Education.* https://www.mediamatters.org/critical-race-theory/unmasking-moms-liberty.

Lubienski, C. (2013). Privatising form or function? Equity, outcomes and influence in American charter schools. *Oxford Review of Education, (39)*4, 398–513. http://dx.doi.org/10.1080/03054985.2013.821853.

Lubienski, C. (2023, January 23). Op/Ed: School vouchers are an impediment to student learning not a panacea for education. *The Indianapolis Star.* https://

www.indystar.com/story/opinion/2023/01/23/school-vouchers-another-education-reform-idea-doesnt-work/69827665007/.

Ludwig, J. (2022, April 23). Opinion: The surprising solution to gun violence. *CNN.* https://www.cnn.com.

Mansfield, E., and K. Jimenez. (2022, October 23). These PACS are funding "parents" rights advocates' running for local school board positions. *USA TODAY.* https://www.usatoday.com/in-depth/news/politics/2022/10/23/super-pacs-spending-local-school-board-races/8125668001/.

Marshall, J. M. (2014). Navigating the religious landscape in schools: Towards inclusive leadership. *Theory Into Practice,* (53), 139–48. doi:10.1080/00405841.2014.887885.

Marples, R. (2014). Parents' rights and educational provision. *Studies in Philosophy and Education,* (33), 23–39. doi:10.1007/s11217-013-9360-9.

McConnell, D. L., and C. E. Hurst. (2006). No "Rip Van Winkles" here: Amish education since *Wisconsin v. Yoder. Anthropology and Education Quarterly, (37)*3, 236–54. https://www.educacaodomiciliar.fe.unicamp.br/sites/www.educacaodomiciliar.fe.unicamp.br/files/2022.

McGraw, M. (2023, January 26). Trump unveils new education policy loaded with culture war proposals. *Politico.* https://www.politico.com/news/2023/01/26/trump-unveils-education-policy-culture-war-00079784.

McLaughlin, L., and R. Hendricks. (2017, February). Intellectual freedom, censorship, and case law. *Teacher Librarian, (44)*3, 8–11.

McWilliam, E. (2008). Unlearning how to teach. *Innovations in Education and Teaching International, (45)*3, 263–69. doi:10.1080/14703229908022176147.

Meckler, L. (2022, December 1). Education wars are fiercest in politically mixed places, survey finds. *The Washington Post.* https://www.washingtonpost.com/education/2022/12/01/school-culture-war-poll/.

Mervosh, S. (2022, August 27). Back to school in DeSantis' Florida, as teachers look over their shoulders. *The New York Times.* https://www.chicagotribune.com/nation-world/ct-aud-nw-nyt-desantis-schools-don't-say-gay.

Mezirow, J. (1997). Transformative learning: Theory to practice. *New Directions for Adult and Continuing Education, (74)*5, 5–12. doi:10.1002/ace.7401.

Molden, D. C., and E. T. Higgins. (2012). Motivated thinking. In Kenneth J. Holyoak and Robert G. Morrison (Eds.), *The Oxford handbook of thinking and reasoning,* 390–412. Oxford, UK: Oxford University Press.

Mozert v. Hawkins County Board of Education. 579 F. Supp. 1051 (E.D. Tenn).

Napolitano, J. (2022, March 23). After losing high-profile book battle, conservative Moms for Liberty turns to critical Tennessee school board race. *The 74.* https://www.the74million.org.

Natanson, H. (2022, July 26). After court ruling, activists push prayer into schools. *The Washington Post.* https://www.washingtonpost.com/education/2022/07/26/school-prayer-kennedy-church-state/.

Natanson, H. (2023a, March 18). Covid changed parents' view of schools—and ignited the education culture wars. *Washington Post.* https://www.washingtonpost.com/education/2023/03/18/pandemic-schools-parental.

Natanson, H. (2023b, May 18). School librarians face a new penalty in the banned-book wars: Prison. *The Washington Post.* https://www.washingtonpost.com/education/2023/05/18/school-librarians-face-new.

Natanson, H., and N. Asbury. (2022, November 17). Va. education board delays review of new history and social studies standards. *The Washington Post.* https://www.washingtonpost.com/education/2022/12/17/va.-board-delays-review.

National Commission on Excellence in Education. (1983). *A nation at risk: The imperative for educational reform.* Washington, DC: United States Department of Education.

National Defense Education Act, PL 85–864 (1958).

Neufeld, B., and G. Davis. (2010). Civic respect, civic education, and the family. *Educational Philosophy and Theory, (42)*1. doi:10.1111/j1469-5812-2008-00506.x.

Parker, T. (nd). Martin Luther King, Jr. "The arc of the moral universe is long, but it bends toward justice" quote or no quote? https://professorbuzzkill.com/martin-luther-king-jr-the-arc-of-the-moral-universe-is-long-but-it-bends-toward-justice-quote-or-no-quote/.

Pekoll, K. (2020, Sep-Oct). Managing censorship challenges beyond books. *Knowledge Quest, (49)*1, 28–33.

Pendarkar, E. (2022, November 4). How to respond to parents' CRT complaints. *Education Week.*

Phi Delta Kappa. (nd). https://pdkpoll.org.

Public Funds Public Schools (PFPS). (2020, March 2). Parents sue Tennessee to block unconstitutional voucher law. https://pfps.org/tennesee-voucher-lawsuit.

Ravitch, D. (2022, April 5). Peter Greene: "Moms for Liberty" are shocked by literal interpretation of "Don't Say Gay" bill. https://dianeravitch.net.

Rebell, M. A. (2014). Poverty, educational achievement, and the role of the courts. *New England Journal of Public Policy, (26)*1, 1–11. http://scholarworks.umb.edu/nejpp/vol26/iss1/7.

Reich, R. (2002, Fall). Opting out of education: *Yoder, Mozert,* and the autonomy of children. *Educational Theory, (52)*4, 445–61. https://www.proquest.com/openview/bac02bfe96fa2758927a03ac42ccf56e/1?pq-origsite=gscholar&cbl=34718.

Reimers, F. (2006). Citizenship, identity, and education: Examining the public purposes of schools in an age of globalization. *Prospects, (36)*3, 275–94.

Richman, T., and C. Smith. (2022, March 3). Bolstered by CRT, book fights, conservative PACs aim to "take back" Texas school boards. *Dallas Morning News.* www.dallasnews.com/education/2022/03/03/bolstered-by-crt-book-fights-conservative.

Rosales, I., and J. Garcia. (2023, May 23). Florida school system has closed investigation into teacher who showed Disney movie with gay character. *CNN.* https://www.cnn.com/2023/05/23/us/florida-teacher-lgbtq-disney-movie-investigation/index.html#:~:text=The%20Hernando%20County%20School%20Board,by%20Jenna%20Barbee%2C%20the%20educator.

Rubin, J. (2022, November 30). Cynical MAGA censors are damaging public education. *The Washington Post.* https://www.washingtonpost.com/magazine/2022/11/30/cynical-maga-censors-are-damaging-public-education.

Russell, B. Z. (2015, March 17). Idaho Senate passes Sen. Mary Souza's parent rights measure. *The Spokesman-Review (Spokane, WA).* https://www.spokesman.com/stories/2015/mar/17/idaho-senate-passes-sen-mary-souzas-parent-rights/.

Salzman, D. (2022). The constitutionality of orthodoxy: First Amendment implications of laws restricting critical race theory in public schools. *The University of Chicago Law Review, (89)*4. https://chicagounbound.uchicago.edu/cgi/viewcontent.cgi?article=6299&.

San Antonio Independent School District v. Rodriguez, 422 US 1 (1973).

Schneider, J. (2019, May 30). Charter schools were supposed to save public education. Why did people turn on them? *The Washington Post.* https://www.washingtonpost.com/news/posteverything/wp/2019/05/30/feature/charter-schools/.

Scott, D. (2014). Knowledge and the curriculum. *The Curriculum Journal, (25)*1, 14–28. http://dx.doi.org/10.1080/09585176.2013.876367.

Sedler, R. A. (2006). From Blackstone's Law duty of parents to educate their children to a constitutional right of parents to control the education of their children. *Forum on Public Policy (2007).* https://digitalcommons.wayne.edu/lawfrp/194.

Sewell, D. (2022, August 28). School district's new leader steps into a CRT hornets nest. *The Cincinnati Enquirer.* https://www.cincinnati.com/2022/08/28.

Shaffer, M. B., and B. Dincher. (2020). In Indiana, school choice means segregation. *Kappan, (101)*5, 40–43. https://doi.org/10.1177/0031721720903827.

Shapiro, E., and B. M. Rosenthal. (2022, September 11). In Hasidic enclaves, failing private schools flush with public money. *The New York Times.* https://www.nytimes.com/2022/09/11/nyregion/hasidic-yeshivas-schools-new-york.

Shaw, J. S. (2010). Education—A bad public good? *The Independent Review, (15)*2, 241–56.

Sikkink, D. (1999, September). The social sources of alienation from public schools. *Social Forces, (78)*1, 51–86.

Slaby, M. J. (2021, July 30). School board meetings turn testy: Gender identity debate disrupts many in county. *Indianapolis Star.*

Slaby, M. J. (2022a, January 26). Public comment returns to Carmel Clay school board with 2 speakers. *Indianapolis Star.*

Slaby, M. J. (2022b, April 4). Candidates to get more support. Hamilton County groups to put money into school boards. *Indianapolis Star.*

Sollenberger, R. (2021, November 7). The aristocrats funding the critical race theory "backlash." *Daily Beast.* https://www.thedailybeast.com/right-wing-aristocrats-fund-critical-race-theory-backlash.

Solochek, J. S. (2021, November 29). Florida parents say they want rights in schools. What does that mean? *St. Petersburg Times (FL).*

Solochek, J. S. (2022, July 15). At Moms for Liberty event in Tampa, a push to win school board elections. *St. Petersburg Times (FL).*

State of Wisconsin v. Jonas Yoder et al., 406 US 205 (1972).

Sternberg, R. J., A. Reznitskaya, and L. Jarvin. (2007). Teaching for wisdom: What matters is not just what students know, but how they use it. *London Review of Education, (5)*2, 143–58. doi:10.1080/14748460701440830.

Stitzlein, S. M. (2015). Addressing educational accountability and political legitimacy with citizen responsibility. *Educational Theory, (65)*5, 563–80.

Stitzlein, S. (2020). The democratic potential of parental dissent: Keeping public schools public, legitimate, and educational. *Educational Theory, (70)*3, 355–72. https://onlinelibrary.wiley.com/doi/abs/10.1111.edth.12429.

Sugishita, J., and R. Dresser. (2019). Social-emotional learning (SEL) in a field course: Preservice teachers practice SEL-supportive instructional strategies. *Journal of Inquiry & Action in Education, (10)*1, 36–67.

Suitts, S. (2016, November). Students facing poverty: The new majority. *Educational Leadership, (74)*3, 36–40.

Suitts, S. (2019, June 4). Segregationists, libertarians, and the modern "school choice" movement. *Southern Spaces.* www.southernspaces.org.

Support CCS. (2023). Our mission. https://supportccs.org/?page_id=1817.

Swensson, J. (2023). *It's all about learning: The struggle in choosing traditional public education or privatization.* London: Rowman & Littlefield.

Swensson, J., J. Ellis., and M. Shaffer. (2019a). *Unraveling reform rhetoric: What educators need to know and understand.* London: Rowman & Littlefield.

Swensson, J., J. Ellis., and M. Shaffer. (2019b). *An educator's GPS: Fending off the free market of schooling for America's students.* London: Rowman & Littlefield.

Swensson, J., and M. Shaffer. (2020). *Defining the good school: Educational adequacy requires more than minimums.* London: Rowman & Littlefield.

Swensson, J., and L. Lehman. (2021). *Reliable school leadership: What all students deserve*. London: Rowman & Littlefield.

Swensson, J., L. Lehman., and J. Ellis. (2021). *The thief in the classroom: How school funding is misdirected, disconnected, and ideologically aligned.* London: Rowman & Littlefield.

Tang, A. (2018). School vouchers, special education, and the Supreme Court. *University of Pennsylvania Law Review,* (167), 337–97.

Terruso, J., and M. Hanna (2021, November 26). The tension and political movement that rose from Pa.'s school board elections might be here to stay. *The Philadelphia Inquirer.*

Weddle, E. (2023, April 27). Behind closed doors, Indiana lawmakers finalize bill to ban books from school libraries. *WFYI.* https://www.wfyi.org/news/articles/behind-closed-doors-indiana-lawmakers-finalize-bill-to-ban-books-from-school-libraries.

Wenneborg, E. (2020). The double bind of parental conscience. *Philosophical Studies in Education, 51,* 44–53.

Wiles, J. R. (2010). Overwhelming scientific confidence in evolution and its centrality in science education—And the public discontent. Science Education Review, (9)1, 18–27.

Willen, L. (2022, March 15). A lesson in hypocrisy—what's really behind the "parental rights" movement. *The Hechinger Report.* https://hechingerreport.org.

Wu, D. (2023, February 10). Ala. schools canceled a black author's visit. Families rallied around him. *The Washington Post.* https://www.washingtonpost.com/nation/2023/02/10/alabama-author-barnes-hoover-school/#:~:text=It%20started%20as%20a%20rumor,February%20for%20Black%20History%20Month.

Yurcaba, J. (2023). Penguin Random House and Florida parents sue school district over book bans. *NBC Out.* https://www.nbcnews.com/nbc-out/penguin-random-house-and-florida-parents.

Index

academic achievement. *See* learning
anarchic dissent, 60–62, 65, 67, 69, 91, 98, 102, 127, 151
arbiters of choice, 6
arc of the moral universe, 19–20, 30, 101, 165

balance-as-equity, 148
book bans. *See* censorship
boutique-ideology, 21–22, 24, 29, 34, 70, 126, 164
Brown v. Board (1956), 20, 66, 118

caregivers. *See* parents
censorship, 29, 40, 43, 49, 57–58, 82, 120, 138
charter schools, 21, 67–68, 72
choice. *See* partisan education
citizenship, 7, 152, 154, 161, 166; education, 10, 101, 143, 145–47, 158, 165, 166; exclusionary, 147; participatory, 7, 14, 18, 40, 50, 67–68, 81, 90, 128, 146–47, 149, 160, 162
civic respect, 5, 102, 144–45, 163, 166
common (public) good, 9, 12, 19, 22, 27, 42, 49, 52, 66, 89, 95, 102, 122, 127, 129, 147, 149, 151, 162–63, 165, 167–68

community, 50, 68, 91, 148; Amish, 43–44, 113, 129–30; Hasidic, 43–44, 113, 129–31
competition, 11, 64, 68, 76–78, 80, 83, 92–93, 95
constitutional democracy, 4, 8–9, 18, 22, 51, 66, 70, 93, 96, 116, 143, 151–52, 160, 166, 168
consumer relations, 21–22, 70, 82, 100, 132, 135
cost avoidance, 102
COVID-19, 20, 24–25, 33, 45
Critical Race Theory (CRT), 30–31, 33, 36, 43, 63, 69, 136
curriculum, 28, 31–32, 36, 100, 115, 119, 126, 130, 144, 158

defunding, 33, 79–80, 101, 132
difficult knowledge, 27, 32, 146

education, 27; adult-centric, 6, 21, 24, 31–32, 49, 59, 64, 88; control of, 6, 15, 22; formal, 14, 19; government intrusion on, 25–26; human flourishing from, 27; informal, 13–14; student-centric, 6, 8, 49, 65, 68, 135
evolution, 67, 107–8

181

faith, 5, 16, 20–21, 29, 39, 41, 46, 90, 107–10, 113, 148, 166; dominionism, 29, 89, 110, 114; evangelism, 16, 29, 89, 110, 114; foundationalism, 47, 97, 114; fundamentalism, 29, 89, 91, 110
fear, 34–37, 44, 50–51, 57, 78, 80, 90, 125
free market education, 11, 72, 78, 82; marketplace metaphor, 21, 31, 77–78; theory, 11–12, 21, 31, 47

good dissent, 137, 146, 151–52, 154; definition of, 151
government, 67, 109, 118–19, 121, 138; compelling interests of, 7, 10, 15, 41–42, 70, 123, 163; freedom from, 65; obligations of, 20, 75, 147; that works, 7, 10, 50, 90, 111, 122, 128, 134, 144, 149, 154, 158–60, 162–63, 167
grooming, 33, 36

how to think, 6, 24, 52, 59, 79, 91, 96–97, 101, 115, 128, 135, 150, 163, 167

ideologue. *See* partisans
ideology, 5, 10, 15, 28, 33, 39, 49, 62, 91, 95, 97, 133; certainties of, 11; definitions of, 87
indoctrination, 10, 26, 35–36, 59, 158
instruction. *See* teaching
intellectual autonomy, 32, 39–40, 58, 75, 89, 96, 123, 146, 151, 162; definition of, 39
intelligence, 27, 39, 150

knowing along with others, 75, 88–90, 95–97, 101, 126, 133, 137, 167–68

learning, 6, 8, 24, 26, 29, 31, 40, 42, 49, 59, 71, 76–77, 81, 89, 91, 93, 95, 126, 143, 148, 157, 161, 167; dumbed down, 132

legislation, 57–58, 67, 75, 80, 91, 96, 146, 157
"Liberty," 20, 39, 50–52, 70, 76, 79, 92–94, 98, 126, 133, 158, 162–64, 166; definition of, 70
Liberty, 6, 70, 144, 153, 161–63, 165, 167–68

majority rule, 51, 163
mechanisms, 21, 49, 72, 81, 91, 101, 111, 113, 132
memory laws, 48
Moms for Liberty, 17, 36, 63, 69, 121
Mozert v. Hawkins, 42, 115, 117

open futures, 149, 165
orthodoxy (in education), 51–52, 70, 93, 125–26, 159
outside world, 6, 10, 15, 28, 42–44, 88, 98, 127, 130, 149, 161

parents, 6, 8, 12–13, 18, 26, 31, 50–51, 62, 80, 95, 98, 121, 125, 134, 136, 153
partisan education, 16, 21, 32–33, 43–44, 50, 75, 78–79, 82, 87–88, 91, 93, 95, 113, 115–16, 121, 123, 133–34, 137–38, 146, 159, 163–64, 169; control by, 26, 45, 77, 134, 162; cost of, 100–101; definition of, 45, 87; ethos of, 97, 147; marketplace for, 12, 21, 45, 48, 72, 80, 92, 97, 132, 134; networks of, 17, 24, 31, 63, 164; shopping for, 21, 50, 125, 127
partisans, 5, 9, 15, 17, 25, 30, 34, 41, 59, 61, 64, 89, 94, 100, 108, 110, 120–21, 127–28, 136–37, 147, 153, 158, 161–62, 164, 167
partisanship, 5, 7, 9–10, 12, 14, 18, 20–21, 23, 26, 29, 35, 39, 45, 47–48, 57, 59, 61, 67, 69, 71, 78, 82, 88, 90, 94, 97, 101–2, 115–16, 122–23, 125–26, 131–32, 136, 153, 158, 161, 166; closely-held beliefs of, 11, 16; cost of, 102; definition of, 23, 62;

ethos of, 15, 21; purpose of, 88; vulnerability of, 90
Political Action Committee (PAC), 33, 58, 69, 98–100
precarious-balance, 1, 8, 10, 14, 42, 75, 92, 98, 123, 127, 143, 146, 151, 159, 162, 165
preemption, 57–58, 79, 83, 96
public, 127, 146; dissonance, 64–66, 69, 127, 151; things, 88, 128–29, 152

reciprocity, 35, 92, 94, 101–2, 145, 152, 159, 166; criterion of, 92
reform, 11, 68, 71–72, 116–17, 125–27, 129
religion. *See* faith
retreat from conscience, 95–97
rights, 9, 35, 42, 50, 71, 75, 82, 92, 100, 144, 148, 151, 158, 166; constitutional, 41, 117–18; parental, 7, 9, 15, 45, 48, 57, 63, 65, 69, 99, 121–22, 134–35
rule of law, 9–10, 42, 66, 101, 122, 128, 145, 159, 162–63

school board, 8, 58–59, 68, 98–99, 120, 138, 153
self-government, 10, 157–59, 163
"self" government, 139, 143, 157–58, 163–64, 169
Shanker, Albert, 12
singularity, 92, 146, 166
smart, 3
Social-Emotional Learning (SEL), 31, 36, 47, 58, 135–36
social reality, 4, 8, 15, 27, 42, 48, 60, 62, 70, 76, 79, 88, 90, 93–94, 127, 133–34, 147, 153, 157, 161, 164–65
standardized testing, 64, 77, 80–81
State of Wisconsin v. Jonas Yoder et al. (1972), 41, 114, 117, 129–30
static-balance, 1, 11–12, 15, 19–20, 27, 48, 68, 75, 89, 123, 153, 159, 166

straw man, 50
students, 1, 3, 18–19, 25–27, 31, 34, 36, 39, 41, 43, 49, 63, 79, 81, 90, 97, 101, 121, 123, 128–29, 135, 137, 149, 158–59, 165, 167

teaching, 28, 30, 32, 39, 42, 81–82, 108, 115, 130, 132, 135, 138, 150, 159, 161, 168
tension of diversity and unity, 7, 162
threats, 17, 34, 39, 41, 44, 52, 90–91, 127
traditional public education, 6, 8–10, 14, 18, 23–24, 26, 34, 41, 48, 62, 68, 75–77, 80, 89, 99, 118, 123, 125, 127–28, 131, 138, 145, 147, 149, 152, 157, 160, 163, 165, 169; control by, 7; cost of, 100; neutrality of, 10, 35, 50, 66, 107, 116, 123, 133, 137, 148, 167; obligation of, 27; purpose of, 5, 7, 14, 24, 29, 70, 115, 117, 123, 134, 143–44, 162, 169
transactional relationships, 87–88, 91, 94–95
two-prong test, 114–16

universal singularity, 5, 12, 20, 23, 42, 48, 51, 65, 76, 87–88, 92, 94, 96–97, 117, 127, 129, 133, 153, 160, 164; definition of, 92
US Constitution, 42, 47, 75, 117–18; First Amendment, 35, 58, 114–15, 117, 119–20, 158; Fourteenth Amendment, 122–23; Third Amendment, 121–22
US Supreme Court, 109, 111, 114, 118, 122, 158, 167

vouchers, 21, 30, 33, 72

what-to-think, 6, 49, 61, 80, 82, 97, 115

About the Author

A teacher, coach, assistant principal, principal, deputy superintendent, and superintendent, Jeff Swensson served for forty-five years in public school districts across the Midwest. He earned his BA from Amherst College, MAT from Northwestern, and PhD from Indiana University. He is the coauthor of five books and the author of another book. His professional interests focus on leadership and instruction in traditional public schools.

www.ingramcontent.com/pod-product-compliance
Lightning Source LLC
Chambersburg PA
CBHW021850300426
44115CB00005B/88